GW01607061

The Wild Geese are Flighting

The Wild Geese are Flighting

John Horsfall

Kineton : Printed by
The Roundwood Press Limited
1976

By the same author

THE IRON MASTERS OF PENNS (1971)

Printed in 1976 by
The Roundwood Press Limited, Kineton, Warwick

Made and printed in Great Britain

To our friends, and adversaries,
who fought in the line in Tunisia,
and whom we left behind us.

Contents

Illustrations

Maps

Acknowledgments

THIS ACCOUNT OF the activities of some of our soldiers in North Africa during Hitler's war would have been a dull and lifeless thing, for me anyway, without the help of a number of my friends and comrades of those days.

I am much indebted to the undermentioned, all of whom have given me their time and put up patiently with tedious cross-examination.

Captain R. J. Robinson, D.C.M., – Robbie, formerly sergeant, and Sid Smith, otherwise Fusilier S. W. Smith 05, both of D Company, have put up with interminable sessions in my office and have contributed much from their own experiences. Robbie has in fact set down in writing some of his patrol actions at considerable length, and both have accepted the searching scrutiny which this narrative has required.

Mr H. W. Baker, – Bert, the medical sergeant, and Leslie Finch, Mr L. T. Finch, B.E.M., late orderly room sergeant, took the trouble to come over and spend an evening with me to help sort out some of our problems.

David Bartlett, our colour sergeant and later company sergeant major of D Company, has written extensively from his home in Northumberland in reply to my letters, and has filled in most of the gaps in my own records.

Dick Jefferies and Desmond Gethin have also written at considerable length. Dick, Brigadier R. C. P. Jefferies, C.B.E., has lately retired. Formerly our adjutant of the Faughs in Tunisia, Dick found D Company vexatious. "I put the telephone down on you once to stop myself being rude and you complained to Beauchamp about it; he was so embarrassed when he felt he had to tell me about it!" Desmond, Major D. R. le P. Gethin, sent me a mass of reminiscences which we eventually sorted out into sequence, Desmond's memory being splendid save for a slight weakness with dates.

Pat Scott wrote, "You have my blessing in advance to make any remarks you like about your C.O. . . ." This from my late commander, now Major General T. P. D. Scott, C.B., C.B.E., D.S.O. Pat later succeeded Nelson Russell as commander of the Irish Brigade. Some of Pat's photographs are included, taken in the course of battle, and he has also supplied valuable comments.

Ian Lawrie, Lt. Col. W. I. Lawrie, D.S.O., M.C., late 17th Field Regiment of 78th Division, has been most helpful in checking artillery data and adding comments of his own. Then a subaltern he and his regiment were extensively engaged in Tunisia from January 1943 onwards, and thereafter with the Irish Brigade for the rest of the war. In the later stages Ian was a battery commander.

Mr Heinz Preussner's help has been absolutely invaluable. Heinz served in Tunisia with Oberstleutnant Koch's 5th Parachute Regiment of the German army, and he has provided most of the colour from "the other side of the hill". The extent of his assistance will I hope be apparent in the narrative. Heinz said that he wished he had come to England sooner. He said it would have been all too easy in 1940 while he waited in Normandy that summer with the rest of the para boys.

Gordon Norwood, our publisher, has spent considerable time and effort in going over this work, out of friendship as well as for professional reasons. As a consequence of his efforts the book's present state is rather different to what it otherwise might have been – if publishable at all.

I have referred in a number of instances to the fascinating writings of the late Brigadier Nelson Russell, C.B., D.S.O., M.C., our former commander of the Irish Brigade, and also to personal letters to me from my C.O. in Tunisia, the late Lt. Col. B. H. Butler, D.S.O., (Beauchamp), who succeeded Pat Scott in the latter part of the campaign. I have also drawn on contemporary letters of my brother officers and other soldiers I served with.

In a way it is a pity that Nelson's writings were so near to the event, as the needs of security prevented inclusion of much important if unpalatable matter, which his splendid wit would have covered so well.

My brother Michael has kindly supplied the photographs of the Tunisian battlefields from his extensive collection of pictures, taken either on operational flights during the battle or immediately afterwards. Although a regular Faugh officer, Mike was then serving in 241 Squadron of fighter bombers. The frontispiece and cover coloured pictures were taken by Mike some years after the war.

I am also much indebted to Messrs The Illustrated London News for their kindness in providing Plate 11, their photograph of Generaloberst von Arnim on his arrival in England in May 1943.

Derek and Eve Archer have also taken the trouble to spend a weekend reading and checking the manuscript. An Inniskilling Fusilier, Derek, Lt. Col. G. D. Archer, is now a serving officer in the Royal Irish Rangers, who unite our three old Irish regiments and preserve the continuity of the Irish Brigade under this slightly different title.

Lastly, and dwarfing all else, there are the efforts of my wife Mary, who has typed the whole book three times and parts of it more than that. She has also done massive editry and applied censorship. "... You *can't* say that ... I absolutely refuse to type this ..." etc.

What would I have done without her?

Foreword

A critic might well ask how, and why, such a story as this was written, and if it was even a true one.

It is of course absolute history, the sources themselves being the reason for writing it. Many of our soldiers are still living, and having the records I owe it to them, and even more to the memory of our friends, to set out for posterity what is perhaps an epic and which otherwise would for ever be lost.

This is the tale of the soldiers of an Irish infantry regiment, some of whom were regulars, some volunteers, and yet others conscripted. The Irish Brigade, to whom they belonged, stole their hearts like the shamrock itself:

> . . . fresh and fair as the daughters of Erin
> Whose smiles can bewitch, and whose eyes can command,
> In each climate that they may appear in . . .

The Irish Brigade was held together by bonds of a kind which were incomprehensible to outsiders, and which grew progressively stronger as the record lengthened. As a fighting formation it had no peer in Hitler's war. It did not give way and its sword was never blunted save by extreme use – and discipline at no time wavered from the old regular standards, however foul the conditions.

I have a complete diary of the events described, written at the time, and the next of kin records of my men. My father and mother in Warwickshire kept all my letters home and there are masses of them, as well as those from my brother officers and other comrades. These include contemporary accounts written in the immediate aftermath of battle, like those of my commanding officer after Kef el Tior. Most touching of all are those in reply to mine from the wives and parents of our casualties, who never once reproached.

But the fact is that war, at least in an infantry regiment, leaves so searing an impact that nothing ever can be forgotten. Even today it is never far from one's thoughts. Nor for that matter are the friends we served with.

The Wild Geese - The Origin

FOR THOSE UNFAMILIAR with Irish history a note of explanation is due.

The term "The Wild Geese" was first used as a cover for the human cargo of ships carrying Irish volunteers into the French service at the end of the seventeenth century.

These Irish soldiers of fortune were the faithful defenders of the Stuart monarchy, but His Majesty King James II died in 1701, and Louis XIV's promise at the deathbed "to sustain the rights of his son" tied the Jacobite interest to that of France for the two ensuing generations, and provided a satisfactory cause for all good Irishmen not already engaged in Queen Anne's service.

In the meantime the imaginative Irish shipping clerks had seen no reason to provoke the servants of Her Majesty with their questionable cargoes of emigrants. They had to describe them as something and they wrote down "Wild Geese".

Conceived in such appealing and memorable circumstances, the title was adopted lovingly by the Irish soldiers of King Louis XIV of France. These were the Wild Geese of ballad and story – The Irish Brigade which gave unequalled service to the cause of France in the time of Marlborough. Sacred to all the Irish regiments this, the most famous of mercenary corps in our national history, was naturally regarded with veneration by the Faughs since our regiment first existed.

I

Prelude

In 1935 the Royal Irish Fusiliers (Princess Victoria's) – the 87th Foot, and known to its friends as the Faughs, differed from the other line regiments.

Not many years previously our politicians had committed the unbelievable folly of disbanding the 18th Foot and the other sacred southern Irish regiments including the Connaught Rangers. We were left from the wreckage, and although we had no regimental home of our own we could recruit freely throughout the length and breadth of the land.

When I was commissioned into the Faughs we were not exactly a regiment at all, but a half of one, our partner being the Royal Inniskilling Fusiliers, who liked to be called the 27th Foot but were usually referred to as "The Skins".

Most of my service was spent in association with the Skins in one form or another. They were always there and it was unthinkable for them not to be. We were pleased when Neville Chamberlain considered that a satisfactory answer to Hitler was to increase the strength of our regular army by several battalions, and that he added one each to our two Irish regiments when carrying out his purpose.

The term "Faugh" was an abbreviation of the regimental war cry "Faugh a Ballagh" – a gaelic expression believed to mean "clear the way". In fact it was intended as "get out of the way" when addressed to Spanish soldiery in the Peninsula, where it first became commonly used. The regiment was then fighting Soult, and others, and had found its allies a nuisance as usual.

The cry thereafter became immortalised at the battle of Barrosa in 1811, when the soldiers of our 2nd Battalion went berserk in a hand to hand struggle with the 8th French Regiment, and overbore them, screaming this battle cry as they did so. According to the poet this expression "Fág an bealach" – of cattle droving, or raiding, origin – gave vent to the most basic primordial emotions in the deep south of Ireland, and it is strange indeed that one day we would experience it ourselves in conditions not so different from those of 5 March 1811.

The officers of the Faughs were mostly Irish, though this was liable to be disputed unless pre-Tudor Irish ancestry could be definitely proven. There was certainly no dispute in the case of our C.O., The O'Donovan, descended from the kings. I of course was obviously a Sassenach and there by accident, so I was accepted as a curiosity.

One and all had joined the Faughs for traditional reasons. Ambition, so far as any of us understood it, was unacceptable, and it was unusual for our officers to be found in staff appointments. They wanted to spend their serving lives with the regiment and they were quite right. It was all that I ever did.

As a consequence of these habits everyone knew each other rather well and there were extensive family connections. Quentin Findlater, when a subaltern, once said that he found it irritating being addressed as "Master Quentin" by N.C.Os. who had served with his father. And even Gus Jefferies was liable to address George French, one of the company commanders, as "Uncle George".

Many of our men were long service, and the Faughs had a way of finding warrant officers and senior N.C.Os. with inherent qualities almost out of this world. Their view about our regiment, and their devotion to it, hardly differed from the feelings of their officers.

Moreover, on mobilisation the regiment was brought to its fighting strength by its reservists, all of whom had already spent at least seven years with the colours, and some fourteen. In consequence it was a stable and serviceable unit that went across the Channel to confront Hitler's hordes. It was not likely to give way.

Another characteristic was the exceptional standard of marksmanship. Brought up in the old way, our soldiers were used to the annual classification. In any case the subject had particular attention in the Faughs, and their ability to shoot with their rifles was scarcely different from the 1914 standards.

I was appointed to command D Company in the summer of 1939, and it could have been a life appointment but for some carelessness four years later. I was then a lieutenant with four years' service, and I owed the honour to the fact that some of my elders and betters had been posted to other commands and functions much against their will. Our country was becoming interested in its soldiers again for the first time since 1918, and regular officers of suitable vintage were in very great demand for the rapidly expanding Territorial Army.

We, the 1st Battalion, were in Guernsey at the time, in that twilight era of peace. There were cocktail parties nightly and the subalterns were detailed in pairs to attend them. It was a pleasant station and almost an idyllic one, but training of any kind was virtually impossible save for shooting on the excellent rifle range on Jersey.

As everyone of that generation knows, there was less apparent tension during the late summer of 1939 than there had been at any time during the previous eighteen months, but I think that everyone knew it to be the last lull before the storm. At the end of August all was peace and serenity until one morning, at breakfast, Alban Low, our second in command, came into the mess and said, "I am sorry, chaps, we have got to be out of the island by nightfall". Our government at least knew the blow was about to fall, and twenty four hours later we found ourselves under canvas at Bulford near the artillery barracks.

I had simply loaded my kit and dog into my car and driven on to the Weymouth boat, leaving most of my property in Guernsey to the tender mercies of a rear party. This was the last I saw of most of it and in consequence, like other brother officers of that period, I had virtually no civilian clothes after Hitler's final elimination. The regimental silver however fared well, as it fell into the hands of the Germans when they occupied the island and, regarding it as near sacred, they treated it with sentimental respect.

The Germans invaded Poland at dawn on 1 September, and we in common with all the armed forces were ordered to mobilise. That evening Lieutenant Gus Jefferies and I drove over to General

Webber's home at Cannington with the regimental colours, the general then being Colonel of the Regiment.

The following morning I was entertaining D Company during the forty eight hours of suspense that preceded the declaration, when a gunner subaltern came over and said, "Come and have a drink, boys, the war's started." In the gunners' mess there were a dozen or so officers busy setting about a crate of champagne, with the usual toasts customary on these occasions – "bloody war and quick promotion, etc. . . ." Charming, but in fact our gunner friends were a day premature.

Later that afternoon the battalion moved to Thame in Oxfordshire, where D Company was billeted in the Workhouse during the mobilisation period.

The following evening Charles O'Farrell and I were sitting on the wall surrounding D Company's abode, discussing what lay before us. Charles, then a lieutenant, was D Company's second in command. I said that I saw this war as a challenge to our generation. Charles, like one or two others I knew, agreed with that thought in principle, but he also said that it would see the destruction of everything that our generation valued, and that he did not suppose many of us would see the end of it. Charles was not usually depressing like that.

The officers were quartered in the Spread Eagle. That night of 3 September there was a very considerable party, interrupted in the late night by Colonel The O'Donovan coming down clad in pyjamas and trench coat – O'D praying the subalterns to allow him the privilege of sleep which he needed even if they didn't.

Three weeks later we were in France, and just as well too.

That is how our war began.

Strictly speaking this is a brief account of some of the activities of D Company, and how it fared when it came to justify its existence. Mainly this is the story of its North African adventures, but the first act of our national drama requires comment, if only for the reason that no serious person writing of the period could possibly ignore it. The disaster which the British Expeditionary Forces suffered in 1940 was the most absolute and total one ever achieved in the whole of our national history since the luckless Harold drew his sword for the last time at Hastings. It was none the less an epic, and I do not think that many British soldiers who served at that time were other than proud to have done so. There were also portents for the future.

The regiment had returned from the French shambles, undismayed but with an utter contempt for anyone who bore the title of "ally". Their feelings were epitomised by a scene in front of B Company when a French soldier flung his rifle down at Quentin Findlater's feet, wailing "C'est fini, tout c'est fini". As Quentin observed, his tired warriors were in no mood to put up with that sort of nonsense, but the incident itself was symbolic in our view of all things French in 1940.

The final manifestations of our regiment's feelings for our late ally occured on the night of the French surrender in June.

The news that night of 17 June 1940 was followed by a spontaneous and massive mess party to celebrate the elimination of the last of our allies. No more defection or treachery, no more association with poltroons and cowards. Now we could fight "an English war" as Dorothy Sayers wrote in her superb poem – though the Faughs might have added, as one of them did, "to preserve the neutrality of Ireland".

Years were to pass before we learned the other lesson, to give our absolute trust to our friends and allies who we knew would never fail us.

The circumstances of the times were conducive to our feelings. The Faughs naturally assumed that other troops would behave as we did, and expected to see them clean and shaven, alert and prepared to fight. When we noticed that these characteristics were lacking with men whose morale had broken, and who had become a rabble, the Faugh reaction to their allies was inevitable, though tempered at the time with sorrow. The revulsion came later when the perfidy of the politicians became known, and with it the realisation that many of the French civil population had thrown in the towel. We saw these signs for ourselves, but we could also remember some dozens of French warriors who did not do so, whose own leaders had vanished and who willingly assigned their fortunes to D Company. These men fought beside us and did not give up. Nor did a pair of their tank crews who died on the bridge at Gorre, these things merely proving that some regiments, and some men, have higher standards than others, and that those who have a sense of honour are not prepared to lose it.

Added to all this were the self-evident signs of military collapse, the orders we were receiving and the conduct of the enemy alike showing how rapidly this was happening. In the course of a few days we had faced east, south, west and north-west. Under these circumstances there was unavoidable disruption in the command system of our own army, though there was no failure of spirit here. We had reached that point which Kipling dwelt on – about conduct when the military shambles was total – and the Faughs undoubtedly found a perverted pleasure in contemplating their surroundings at that time, and recognising the challenge. It was comforting to have such convincing proof of our regiment's morale in this evil period.

However there were some people who could still show us up. On 27 May D Company was ordered to an obscure place called Lestrem, with instructions to defend the river bridges until either the survivors of the 4th Infantry Brigade, or the Germans, arrived, acting suitably according to which of them came first. On reaching the place we found the brigadier and his staff relaxing in deck-chairs. He expressed delight at seeing us and pressed me to a drink. He went on to say that two of his battalions were destroyed and the remainder surrounded, and that vast forces of tanks and German infantry were pressing up the road towards them. Until our arrival the valiant brigadier, the brigade major and a few others were preparing themselves for the role of Horatius. After giving me this news we had another cognac or two together before setting to work. Shortly afterwards the German infantry came through the crops opposite, carrying their rifles at the high port – a perfect textbook picture.

The 1st Faughs had some reason for self confidence, and D Company certainly had.

In those last few weeks our fusiliers had learned many things. They discovered that fatigue was an attitude of mind, and that sleep was even a luxury ; that well concealed, and shooting calmly and deliberately at the enemy, eventually he stopped shooting at you – and even went away altogether. They learned about life and death. Some of them discovered the need for alertness having allowed a Hun company to start breakfasting in their midst. All experienced the mysterious tensions which come when the last refugee and the last cart has gone, and the last fragments of rabble passed through, that once was a part of the army of France – and one lay awaiting the enemy.

Several events of importance to D Company had occurred in the intermission before the war became personal. The O'D, much lamented, departed to unsought promotion and Guy Gough, equally venerated, came in his stead. Charles O'Farrell was posted to our carrier platoon, a unit principally intended for reconnaissance and equipped with light armoured track vehicles – vexatious machines of indifferent performance which for some reason always seemed to fascinate their owners.

Gus Jefferies came to D Company as second in command, for the remainder of his brief life. Another case of "Whom the Gods love. . . ."

Humour was rarely absent in an Irish regiment even during a German blitzkrieg, and sometimes our warriors showed excess of zeal. Quinlan, my driver, and I think Clanachan, then 18 Platoon's orderly, arrested and marched in to my presence, among others, the divisional chief of staff. They said that the unfortunate colonel had been asking Fusilier Harvey suspicious questions. The "others" included the local French level-crossing keeper.

The drivers were much in the limelight during these three wild weeks as they provided the only means of communication, field telephones being utterly useless in that rapidly moving battle. Corporal Cooper, my M.T. corporal, and Fusilier Quinlan, ran all our messages to battalion headquarters in our eight-hundred-weight trucks, and in our five-day battle on the La Bassée canal provided a daily source of amusement for the German gunners on the slag heaps opposite. Finally these gentlemen achieved a direct hit on one of our machines. A poor one anyway and no loss, as the corporal cheerfully observed. The driver survived.

On the third day of the battle we had run out of ammunition, and Cooper came back with another fifteen thousand rounds – and a case of claret for his company commander with the compliments of Chips Davies, then regimental second in command.

We also heard at last from Desmond Gethin and his redoubtable henchman Sergeant Martin. After two days of incessant musketry from, and into, 17 Platoon, we were getting anxious, until out of the dark night came Fusilier McGee 03 bearing messages. McGee was breathless with excitement, having wormed his way past the opposition pickets. The text of Desmond's message read, "Any chance of some food? We're getting bloody hungry".

In the last days the 1st Faughs made back for Dunkirk like the rest of the B.E.F., D Company among them – still seventy strong, though thirty fewer than at the start of the battle. When we so ill-advisedly went into Belgium, Second Lieutenant Michael Connell had been posted in to us by some humourist, as supernumerary, "for instruction". Well, instruction he had certainly had, and supernumerary or not he was welcome now, equally to Desmond and to me, as we alone remained of the officers. Known generally as "Crow", I think he owed his strange title to one of Gus Jefferies' christenings, and admittedly he looked vaguely bird-like.

As we moved back through the blazing débris of that dive-bomber's paradise I observed to our junior subaltern, "I hope, Crow, you realise your distinction, that you are now taking part in the biggest shambles ever achieved by our army in the whole of its history." Crow remarked that yes, he agreed all this, but that he didn't suppose it would be the end of the matter.

Talking to our warriors afterwards, their attitude was clear enough. This was but a prelude.

Prelude or not, the afterthoughts lingered permanently. We could respect, and even admire, our enemy as soldiers, but no single thing had happened in the Battle of France that left us in any doubt or fear of the outcome when next we met them.

2

The Wild Geese are Flighting

THE COMPANY'S DEPARTURE from Dalmellington may not have been a dignified one but it would have an honoured place in the local mythology.

Wildly hilarious, hardly a man was sober – either among soldiers or townsfolk – and the Provost himself set the example, determined that this, the last fling of his people, should be beyond either restraint or reproach. More than this, it was an orgy – of truly Roman dimensions, and it might even have satisfied Nero save that the participants actually stopped short of burning the town down.

A worse timing could hardly have been chosen by the unperceptive movements staff – 10 p.m. on a Saturday night in an Ayrshire mining village where we had lived as a part of the community for three months past.

It had been a happy three months. Pat Scott, the C.O., had sent us there as the hill terrain was ideal for the types of field training which we had in mind, and he was no doubt influenced by my having rented a nearby grouse moor.

That grouse moor was not to be ignored. Rented for £20, during that autumn it produced over fifty brace of grouse and as many mountain hares, which contributed materially to the wartime diet in our homes. It also embellished the officers' and sergeants' messes of D Company, and enabled a level of princely hospitality which our brother officers in the other companies regarded as an outrage.

We were less successful with fish. Mother wrote, "That salmon you sent . . . the stationmaster telephoned to come and collect it else it would walk out of the station itself."

For three months our warriors had been on and over the lowland hills, and as we were provided with unlimited supplies of every variety and type of ammunition, and were quite unrestricted in its use, they had achieved a standard of excellence in weapon efficiency, both by day and by night, which no regular regiment could ever have attained in peace time. No doubt this was intended by our far-sighted chiefs.

I was pretty sure that most of the fighting ahead of us would be in darkness and so we went out at dusk into the hills, night after night, firing at figure targets stuck into the mountain side – an interesting firework display for the locals with the hills lit up by Very lights and parachute flares, with tracer streaking in all directions. Disturbing for the grouse, but they stuck it out.

We also practised control of our men moving over those dark hills at night; and night attacks, and we learned the colossal scope for confusion when doing them. And we taught them to stalk men silently.

We also discovered who could safely throw grenades, and who couldn't. "Throw the bloody thing, you gobshite," yelled Sergeant Martin, "pretend it's a cricket ball." Then under his breath, hissing, "Fat lot of good talking to you about cricket, you horror from Cork."

In the evenings the village took us to their hearts. Writing to my brother Michael about our hosts, I said, ". . . The warriors are – excited. That last dance was a terrific success. Irish dancing in a big way and did it much better than the locals did their Scottish dance, 'The Drops of Brandy' – at the conclusion the pipe major got completely bottled, fell down the steps and had to be carted off to hospital. . . ."

And to my mother, "We all loved Dalmellington. Terrific party before leaving. The folks there all said exceptionally nice things about the company. Sorry I shan't be able to supply any more grouse this year."

When we came to leave they had their own ideas of what was fitting to send us on our way. It may not have been honorific, and it may have been partly spontaneous, but it came from the heart and it was not to be forgotten.

None the less the men were drunk, and they and our friends the townsfolk were making so much noise that the embarkation of our hundred warriors in to the buses parked in the square was a military operation horrible to contemplate – and worse to carry out. It was achieved largely by violence, for in accordance with the best Irish practice those of our warriors who were not singing were fighting.

The officers were not drunk, nor was Sergeant Major Wilson – and nor were the police. The combination and teamwork of these few was effective. Our devoted troops were seized from the embraces of their inebriated hosts and literally pitched in to the buses, where they were silenced by our subalterns Chug Sutcliffe and Nick Jefferies, who simply clocked them on the chin in most cases as they came aboard. We owe it very largely to the police that we got away at all that night.

It was quite a long drive to Glasgow Station on that bright and frosty November night in 1942, and it was further still in the troop train down to the Mersey. But it was not long enough for D Company of the 1st Faughs. One has to confess that when they embarked in the good ship *Tegelberg* to leave our shores, many of them for the last time, they were suffering from hangovers only equalled in 1940 when an obliging French host provided them with apple brandy in lieu of cider.

The *Tegelberg* was a comfortable solid Dutch liner of about 12,000 tons, and she left nothing to be desired. Her officers and ship's staff provided us with every courtesy and attention that could have been expected in a liner in peacetime. Our regiment was much impressed.

I shared a cabin with Pat Scott and Peter Murphy. Pat was adjutant when I first joined the regiment. Now he was my C.O., and in later days would be my brigade commander.

We knew each other all too well. Pat has always had a cynical sense of humour well adapted for dealing with our artful and imaginative soldiers. He was very good at perceiving men's motives, and he was not ruffled by circumstances however foul. Also no one could ever have exercised more care and forethought than he did when committing his troops to battle. In consequence there was never a lack of confidence under Pat's command, even if he was called every name in the book behind his back.

Peter commanded A Company. He combined the military virtues with the richest and certainly most hilarious vocabulary that I ever heard used in the army by an officer, and also, like a number of my other and closest friends, he saw no virtue in abstinence. Peter could be relied upon to lift any mess party rapidly to a climax, and when in full cry Alcoholics Anonymous could safely have regarded him as a star candidate. The mess staff regarded him with fascinated horror. During the last year Peter had been relatively quiet, but sometimes I wonder what would have happened had he survived the war. I do not think he tried very hard to do so, and we thereby lost one of our best wits, as well as a colourful and endearing character.

The convoy swung wide into the Atlantic, and headed south over a winter ocean which could scarcely have been kinder to us. The scene was peaceful enough, though the ceaseless activity of the destroyers was a constant reminder that the naval conflict was still far from won.

Entertaining a ship load of troops has been an age-old problem with our army and, so far as D Company was concerned, its solution was largely left in the hands of Hugh Holmes, who was second in command of the company.

Hugh was admirable at lectures. He could convey an air of absolute authority on virtually any subject whether he had previous knowledge of it or not. No doubt he acquired this useful trick as a beak at Sherborne. I do not know if it worked with schoolboys but it certainly impressed our soldiers, and he could combine instruction and entertainment in a manner always worth listening to. He discoursed to the company on Roman and other ancient Mediterranean histories, on geography, and on the unpleasing habits of the Arab residents of the land that lay ahead of us. He also talked on less dainty, and other, purely military subjects.

Hugh was a born instructor, and his capacity in that field was equalled by his ability as an administrator. These were his true roles rather than as the embattled leader of the forlorn hope which I suspect he would have preferred. He was of course the ideal second in command. His normal mode of addressing himself to our soldiers was by the title of "dear boy", which at least provided a pleasing contrast to the four adjectival expressions of Wilson the C.S.M. When the company were not listening to Hugh, they spent their time with their interminable gambling.

It would have been a tedious voyage but for the pleasant companionship.

So we sailed on, over a placid sea and under a starry night sky. Here Nicolas asserted himself to the lasting benefit of many of us. Nick knew his stars – in more respects than one; and in the evenings, after dinner, he went to the trouble of ensuring that the rest of us knew something of them too.

I never see the North Star, Orion and the others, without thinking of Nick Jefferies.

The three platoons which composed D Company were numbered 16, 17 and 18. Nicolas, that is Lieutenant Nicolas Jefferies, commanded 16 Platoon. I never knew anyone quite like Nick; always elegant and perfectly turned out, he invariably showed a sublime indifference to his surroundings, and he secured his soldiers' devotion by methods impossible for other officers. He disguised his exceptional talents with that languid manner fashionable in the eighteenth century, and he had an endearing way of addressing his men, which often included remarks thrown in about his horror at having to associate with them. They found him enchanting. He was liable for instance to request his sergeant to send for a scented handkerchief when doing a foot inspection. For some reason this pose of his seemed to please them, and life in 16 Platoon was rarely a dull one.

Nicolas did not get on terribly well with very senior officers outside our regiment. He tended to take offence at the mere sight of them and they could hardly be expected to like his rather direct remarks, or his capacity for replying in kind to the implication of criticism. Nick had considerable power of expression and never hesitated to use it, no matter to whom, or however exalted. But he never did this to me. Nick and I always saw eye to eye, and there was never a vestige of trouble within the regiment, where Nick's loyalties were lodged firmly and perhaps exclusively. Life with Nicolas was a partnership, and a very pleasant one too. He was D Company's right arm.

Above the regiment I think that Nicolas recognised only the Almighty, knowing perfectly well that he was shortly to meet Him.

This attitude to higher authority was perhaps a tendency with Irish regiments, and any ham-handedness by visiting officers made trouble certain. In a way it was inevitable among those of us who had had the good fortune to be brought up under commanders like Pat Scott and Beauchamp Butler – or The O'Donovan and Guy Gough, my former C.Os. None of them ever criticised save in the kindest way, and one and all made a point of hearing out their subordinates – without feeling in the least obliged to heed what they said.

I made a bad start in this respect, having the distinction of nearly losing my commission on my first day's service.

I was appointed secretary of the Bordon shoot within hours of joining the Faughs, and being sent down to the garrison school for a meeting of the regimental representatives the first person I had encountered was the brigade commander. He was clad in gardening attire. Not knowing him from Adam I assumed that he was one of the gamekeepers. The brigadier did not introduce himself to me, but instead shot a lot of questions at me which I judged to be offensive, and said so.

The next morning I was hauled in front of the C.O., Colonel Tommy Gregg, who asked me what on earth I had done to upset the brigadier. He had apparently said to Tommy that I must leave immediately. So I explained. Tommy Gregg exploded. "Stupid old fool. I knew it was something like that. Don't you worry," – this to his latest joined second lieutenant. I know that there was quite a disturbance afterwards at brigade headquarters, but Tommy had nothing to lose as he was retiring shortly – not that this would have made the slightest difference to his attitude.

Nicolas was supported in his role by Sergeant Fred White, who was the platoon sergeant of 16 Platoon. He was a dapper and polite man, though granite underneath. Fred's disposition had some of the characteristics of his unusual commander, and he and Nick were admirably matched. Commonly known as "Chalky", Fred had considerable clerical talent which was unusual in Faugh N.C.Os. Also in the platoon, commanding one of the sections, was one of the company's private gunmen, Lance Sergeant

Brandon. Brandon was Fred's stand-in, and he would have done well in a saloon fight in the wild west, both as to looking the part and to his capabilities with small arms. He was also temperamentally suited to quelling violence rapidly and efficiently.

17 Platoon was in the care of Lieutenant Douglas Walsh. Douglas had succeeded Desmond Gethin, who had recently been elevated to second in command of B Company, whose officers at the time included my brother Michael and Tommy Wood, and an exceptional sergeant major, Corny Walsh* who, to use Desmond's words, managed to keep some sort of order among them. While there was no doubt as to Douglas's military qualities the appointment to a line regiment made me wonder, as he was about fifteen years older than the rest of the subalterns. However Douglas soon showed that he was just as durable as they were. Sergeant "Crimes" Martin, his platoon sergeant, was equally venerable, aged over forty with twenty-one years' regular service behind him. His regimental diminutive was exploited perhaps by Desmond, but by anyone else at their peril. These two made a solid pair with convincing authority, but the effect was rather spoiled as the next in line of succession was Corporal Robbie Robinson. Robbie was eighteen having, as was then customary among our soldiers, stretched the truth over his age when he enlisted.

According to Robbie, and supported by the not too certain testimony of Fusilier Sid Smith 05, their sergeant owed his strange title to an overcolourful conduct sheet achieved during his first seven years with the colours. On his second engagement Martin evidently saw the light, and put his considerable weight of character behind the forces of law and order. The benefits of this accrued to D Company in Martin's majestic performance during his third engagement, which was the period when we, perhaps fortunately, first knew him. Robbie also remarked that he thought that the change of heart was mainly achieved by the influence of his sergeant's very charming Scots wife.

Lieutenant Chug Sutcliffe, aged twenty-one, had 18 Platoon. A slight figure, he had the enthusiasm of an overgrown schoolboy and was an absolute delight. He was game for anything and he had

*Not to be confused with Douglas.

the gift of finding, and showing, pleasure in whatever he happened to be doing, however tedious it might have seemed to others. 18 Platoon was the joy of his life, and I have no doubt that they found Chug as exhilarating as we did. Chug was my principal shooting companion when we pursued our grouse over the Ayrshire hills, and with his natural eye and aptitude for this kind of sport he very rapidly became an excellent shot.

Chug had another good man in Murphy, his sergeant. Entirely unlike in temperament to the other mercurial members of his ilk that I have known, Sergeant Murphy was a quiet man ; but he had his way with his men in spite of this characteristic and he was well adapted to his lively commander. There was another N.C.O. in 18 Platoon with unusual qualities. Corporal Bartram's role in 18 Platoon was not far different from that of Brandon. Bartram also had outstanding ability with small arms, and the temperament to match it.

To complete the sketch of the principal actors, the C.S.M. was Tug Wilson, a violent and explosive character who scarcely ever used a polite expression where the opposite would serve. He had been signal platoon sergeant until recently, first coming in to prominence when Gus Jefferies was the signals officer. Gus appreciated that kind of character and, with his liking for mimicry, exploited Wilson's extensive vocabulary at every opportunity, so that in Gus's régime most of the battalion became acquainted daily with his sergeant's latest utterances to his flock. Gus's acolytes usually became famous – and Wilson did so above all others.

Colourful or not, Tug Wilson was a good C.S.M. and above average as an administrator. Nothing slipped, but though I did not then realise it he was near his limit, and driving himself. His temper frayed in consequence.

Our colour sergeant, David Bartlett, had been with us for years, and was another character whom most of the regiment knew well. David was the officers' mess corporal during our time in the Channel Islands, and so was very well acquainted with his officers – having had endless opportunity of seeing us at our worst. He was appointed sergeant of 16 Platoon at the outbreak of war, and after Bert Martin was hit in our first action David found himself commanding it for the rest of the Battle of France. David never caused anyone a moment's worry. He was another "quiet man" who just got on with things.

Our idyllic journey was interrupted in the Straits. In the late evening, opposite Gibraltar, our consort to starboard put her helm over, and with neither warning nor apparently any attempt at evasive action by either ship, drove smartly in to *Tegelberg's* side at fifteen knots.

My recollection is that there was little noise or fuss; only a crunching sound which went on for rather a long time and which was followed by the dull roar of surging water, like the noise of a distant train on the London Underground. The alarm bells went of course, but as we had been through the drill daily, falling in at the boat stations had become a habit.

However this time the movements of the ships were interesting. The two drifted apart and the *Tegelberg* sat on the water like an injured duck. Her bows started to dip and she began to heel – steadily. When I had reached the point of speculating as to whether she was in fact going over – and for how long one could stay upright on deck – she stopped, and then equally slowly began to right herself. Our Dutch friends had clearly been busy below. However her bows remained only a few feet above the sea.

After a while power was resumed, and slowly we backed stern first, ignominiously, into Gib, passing our battered colleague on route, who had no bows left.

The last time I set foot in Gibraltar was equally ignominious. We had been put ashore on the first day of 1937 with our friends the Northumberland Fusiliers, to march round the Rock and eliminate the deplorable after-effects of spending New Year's Eve with them. We were then returning from Palestine in the good ship *Athenia* – alas, the first ocean casualty of Hitler's war.

This time, also, we spent only a day there. Time enough to fill the hole in *Tegelberg's* side with cement, but not enough to replace the equipment lost in her submerged forward compartments. These included our motor bikes and some of our weapons, but ammunition was damaged also, including the vital tracer which was indispensible for night fighting.

We slunk out of Gib that night on our own, and at a crawl. In consequence another three days elapsed before we put in to that regrettable Algerian sub-port of Bougie, picking our way through the wrecks which littered its approaches and well behind the rest of the Irish Brigade. Nelson Russell, our brigadier and also a Faugh, was not pleased, and said so with remarks being flashed about as to why his own regiment always contrived to be late for everything except parties.

We spent a day or two in the orange groves behind Bougie, and it was only here that we at last knew the state of affairs in Tunisia, three hundred miles to the east. Here we learned of the Hampshires' gallant but costly stand at Tebourba, and knew that after that lost battle there was only a handful of intact troops left to contain a well stirred up hornets' nest.

In the meantime our warriors ate too many half-ripe oranges and suffered in consequence.

3

Private War

An air of unreality hung over the regiment during the few peaceful days which remained to us. We had landed finally on 10 December and were on our way eastwards three days later.

13 December was a Sunday. Pat Scott called the battalion together for a church service and read the first chapter of Joshua as the lesson ; and very appropriate too. "Be strong and of a good courage. . . " and "There shall not be any man able to stand before thee. . . " This was fine, and from Pat's point of view so too was the concluding "Whosoever shall rebel against thy commandment and not hearken unto thy words in all that thou commandest. . ."

There were no atheists that I knew of in D Company ; nor for that matter, I believe, in the whole of the regiment then. If church services were compulsory our men still went because they wanted to. Fear, resolution, comradeship – all went hand in hand in this, but above all they knew, or soon discovered, that they could not cope on their own without the Divine power to help them. Later, especially with our famous padre Dan Kelleher, these services were uplifting in the highest degree for men who had been badly shaken in battle. When Dan was displeased he could promise Hell to those who performed indifferently and disgraced the Holy cause they were fighting for.

I was seriously worried by the attitude of our men. They seemed to me unduly flippant and quite unable to realise what lay ahead of them. Perhaps the Algerian sunshine and their time in the *Tegel-*

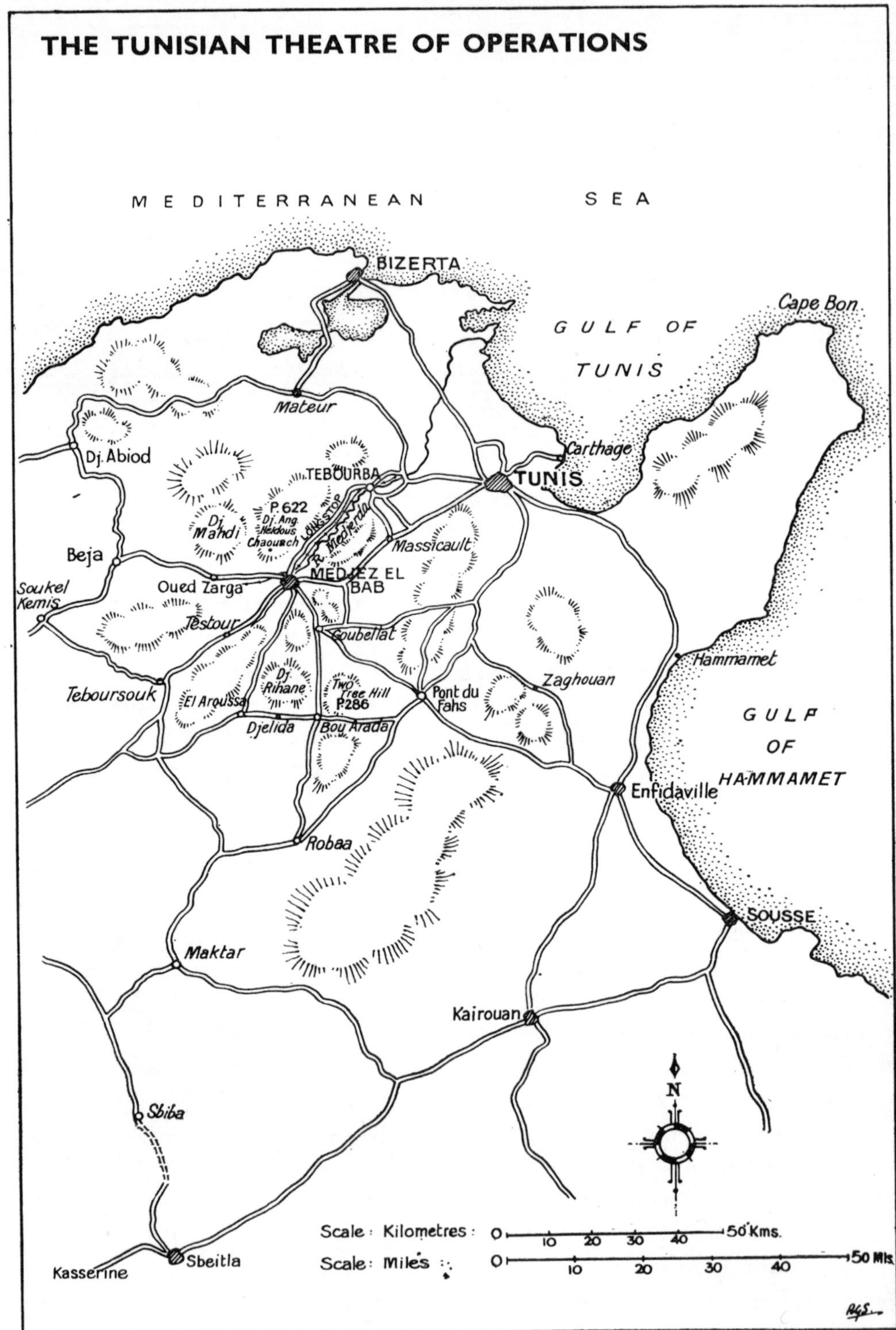
THE TUNISIAN THEATRE OF OPERATIONS
MEDITERRANEAN SEA
BIZERTA
GULF OF TUNIS
Cape Bon
Mateur
Dj. Abiod
TEBOURBA
TUNIS
Carthage
P.622
Dj. Ang.
Heidous
Chaouach
Dj. Mahdi
LONGSTOP
R. Medjerda
Massicault
Beja
Soukel Kemis
Oued Zarga
MEDJEZ EL BAB
Testour
Goubellat
Hammamet
Teboursouk
El Aroussa
Dj. Rihane
Two Tree Hill
P.286
Pont du Fahs
Zaghouan
Djelida
Bou Arada
GULF OF HAMMAMET
Enfidaville
Robaa
SOUSSE
Maktar
Kairouan
N
Sbiba
Scale: Kilometres: 0 10 20 30 40 50 Kms.
Scale: Miles 0 10 20 30 40 50 Mls.
Kasserine
Sbeitla

berg had induced the feeling that it was all just fantasy, and that motoring later through the Algerian hills was only a picnic. With this in mind I said to Pat Scott that I could not predict their conduct when the shock of action hit them. I also mentioned that I would welcome at least an interlude with German aircraft en route, if only to condition them mentally to their purpose in being in this unfriendly land.

Pat merely remarked testily that he hoped to God there would be no such thing, and that all he personally wanted to do was to get them safely in the line, and no doubt thereafter they would do all that was necessary – as indeed they and their forebears always had done.

Over half the company had fought in the Battle of France and they should have known better. That period was exciting, brief and intense, and even if they had taken a conspicuous part in the worst defeat that our army had yet experienced they were quite unmoved by it. They knew that they had been among the first soldiers of our country to encounter the much admired Rommel, then an obscure general commanding the 7th Panzer Division, and they had had the satisfaction not only of stopping his elated and over-confident warriors in their tracks, but had actually killed quite a number of them. They also knew that they could have gone on doing so had they been left to it.

The rest of the company, and all the officers other than myself, were new to battle, but they were not new to each other and the team was united enough.

However I recorded then that our regulars showed a distinct lack of enthusiasm and confidence in other formations – an introspective habit which would change in the months ahead. I said to my father, "I know that the warriors will put up a darn good show and they are intensely keen. It is useful having the French campaign as experience, but nothing could ever be like that again, and one gets some exultation in taking part in something which we know we will win – very different from Dunkirk when we felt that we were the only sound rock in a flood of disaster."

Our regulars had not forgotten their last experience and they trusted no one but themselves.

In a way these were comforting thoughts and the self-reliant feeling was a good one. But it was very near to being one of complacent smugness, a fault to which the Faughs were prone alike by tradition and inclination – and it could lead us into trouble if not closely watched. The Skins always said of their Faugh brothers that we habitually looked down our noses at all other regiments. However I did not notice much difference in their own behaviour.

On 17 December we brewed up tea, the company and the rest of the battalion tucked away on the roadside by an outlandish place called Tebour Souk, about forty miles from Tunis. We stayed here while waiting for Pat's instructions. I recall chatting to Hugh and Sergeant Major Wilson, and observing that in all likelihood this was the last peaceful meal we could expect for some time. We were joined for tea by Major Beauchamp Butler, our regimental second in command, and Charles O'Farrell the adjutant. Charles himself was a D Company graduate and had been second in command of the company at the beginning of the war.

However Beauchamp had dropped in for other things besides tea, and he indicated our concentration area ahead. Also he added by way of afterthought that we had better be ready to defend it.

So, tea concluded, we pushed on to that slab of a mountain in front of us, in intermittent rain squalls. As we arrived we encountered a reception committee of several Me. 109s., who gave a low level aerobatic display around us, fired aimlessly into the hillside, and then departed into the gathering darkness.

We selected suitable tactical positions, dug ourselves in, fed ourselves and generally settled down for the night on the assumption of becoming nocturnal creatures for the next few months.

After a while Beauchamp came to see us again to check that we were quite happy. Pat meantime was conferring with the brigadier. Beauchamp was an Inniskilling by birth, but was as much at home with us as we were with him. He, like others of my friends in their different ways, had a personality perfectly adapted to the mercurial temperament of our Irish soldiers, though his manner belied the rock beneath. He was sensitive and bashful, and he tended to blink and to stutter when giving us unpalatable instructions. I recall no criticism from him ever, but when things were wrong he took all blame on himself. He was a delight to serve under and he was a staunch friend.

We had now arrived at long last, and as we could expect to meet the opposition at any moment, the main subject of interest to all of us was what they had been up to, and were now contemplating.

We do not know all of Hitler's thoughts in November 1942 when he first appreciated the nature of the allied landings in North Africa. But we know what he did, and the speed with which he reacted.

However, two factors stand out which he must have considered.

First, win the U-boat war and the Allied African forces were cut flowers in a vase, and in German eyes at the end of that desperate year they were in a fair way to winning it. No other issue was the equal of this one, for all else hung upon it.

Secondly, the strategic position of the German forces in Africa was radically altered with Alamein just fought, and disastrously lost, only a few days previously. The desert front was now no longer tenable and concentration was inevitable. The Tunisian bulge was the only territory where this was possible and, using such a springboard, the German army could hit back and restore all that had been lost – just as Rommel himself had done at the other end of the front twice already. Moreover the country itself was a ready-made fortress, and whoever held it held also the Mediterranean sea routes.

With such perfect access for rapid reinforcement, and flying time that could be measured in minutes, the Germans knew that Tunisia was theirs for the asking. General Walther Nehring, the first theatre commander, was accordingly ordered to seize the whole of the country. He sent in the 5th Parachute Regiment under Oberstleutnant Koch to form the first bridge-head on 11 November, three days after the allied invasion, and arrived himself on the 14th.

No reaction could have been faster than that, and the Führer disclosed his strategic appreciation by these immediate decisions.

Koch's men were received amicably in the first instance by the local French forces, and the first day was spent in discussion while the latter telephoned for instructions as to which side they were on. After receiving their orders the French expressed their regrets to the oberst and were immediately set upon by his paratroopers who drove them from the district after quite a savage battle.

The German programme was in full swing within a week of the allied landings. They were now committed, and no withdrawal would be possible hereafter without loss of dignity and much else, all of it intolerable to the Führer. In the meantime Rommel's men were racing back from the western desert, compelled alike by their calamitous defeat and the need to join up with their comrades on the Tunisian frontier as fast as ever possible.

There were pre-requisites for German victory: the air space over Tunisia and the Sicilian channel had most certainly to be held, and sufficient forces had to be supplied to defend the passes and outfight the British.

The prospects seemed excellent and the Germans poured troops into the country, landing over twenty thousand men in the first fortnight. Nehring could easily see that the elimination of two or three of those British infantry brigades which spearheaded the allied attack might even end the matter altogether – with gorgeous visions of perhaps the whole expeditionary force in the bag at the end of it, Americans and all.

As for the French, they could be relied upon to run true to form and would change sides once more against the detested British as soon as they saw how matters lay – a point made quite clear already by the conduct of the Governor General when the German forces first landed.

Thus the German thoughts; perhaps. But there was still that sea war to win, and it was a pity they needed so much of their army in Russia.

Another factor was the assumption that Hitler was still winning the war; but thoughtful officers like Generalfeldmarschall Erwin Rommel could be pardoned for having doubts.

Our post-war historians have written much about the German folly of throwing an army away in Tunisia when they could have saved it, but they could hardly have abandoned Rommel, and a win-or-die decision had to be made on the 8th of November of 1942.

The enemy were proved wrong by events, but the German view seems to have had scant attention. Hitler was not mad on that occasion, and had Von Arnim, who succeeded Nehring, handled his forces less wastefully and more circumspectly, in my humble opinion the Germans could have brought the North African war to a stalemate, with incalculable consequences for the subsequent course of the war in Europe.

It poured solidly for the next four days and we were most uncomfortable, not then being used to such things after the pleasures of Dalmellington. However, the Almighty had intervened on our behalf, though we did not then fully realise it, or understand the imperative need for the Germans to overcome our handful of troops at the outset. As it was their tanks were bogged, like ours, in the cement-like Tunisian mud.

At this stage our army in Tunisia consisted of two attenuated divisions – the 6th Armoured to which the Irish Brigade temporarily belonged, and the embattled and depleted 78th Division, of whom the 11th Infantry Brigade and, in particular, its attached 2nd Royal Hampshire Regiment, were so badly battered at Tebourba that further offensive action was hardly practicable for the time being. So we had, in effect, five British infantry brigades scattered round a seventy-mile arc which contained twice their number of angry Teutons, all in a compact mass. Moreover the Germans had not underrated us, and had taken the precaution of shipping over some of the best formations of their army, containing thoroughly dangerous and resolute infantry regiments hand picked for the purpose.

After the 78th Division's repulse at Tebourba our people did the obvious thing of holding the few key features which controlled the routes westwards. The rest of the hills, and the long north-south Goubellat plain in particular, were free to both sides. In practice this meant free to the Germans, as they had far more men. The sector included Djebel Abiod, near the northern coast, down through Medjez el Bab to Bou Arada in the south, and further south again reaching round to the north-east of Robaa, where the ill-equipped French colonial forces under General Juin covered our mountainous southern flank.

Some people may have liked Tunisia, but personally I detested the place, though it was ideal for defensive fighting with its mountain barriers dividing the land. Nelson Russell said that he thought "Tunisia a fine country and couldn't think why our forefathers bellyached about the far east when there were better places at our front door". However I think that few who had spent any time in those rock-bespattered mountains would have agreed with him, and if asked they would no doubt have said that Tunisia was a Hell's brew of a country with few redeeming features. I could never understand how Nelson could write so rapturously, but as he put pen to paper after the sack of Tunis perhaps he was bewitched.

For the most part the uplands of Tunisia were semi-desert, and this also applied in the foothills down to the 1000 foot level or even lower. There may have been other more attractive areas like those of the cork forests, but these desert-like conditions generally existed in the zone of fighting outside the low ground. This state of affairs was due to the combined effects of the climate, and neglect by the Berber inhabitants spread over the fourteen centuries since the Roman power failed, and most of all by the destructive habits of the Arabs and their revolting goats.

Due to their activities, and putting nothing back into the land, all the top soil had long since vanished from the high hills. Washed down in to the plains, or away altogether during the savage winter storms, the low ground had a silt-like consistency which was no doubt exceedingly fertile, and this was where most of the attractive French farms were dotted about.

Unfortunately for our regiments of the line, strategic necessity usually ensured that the principal battles were fought out amongst the highest hills of the theatre, and Tunisia was no exception to this unpleasant impulsion. The mountain area north of Medjez el Bab dominated the entire campaign, and it was so foul, broken, blasted and inhospitable that the Devil himself was surely the principal agent in its creation. This was the district that evoked Pat Scott's cri de coeur, "My God, if we ever get out of this place alive we can talk about it for the rest of our days."

The German command of the air to begin with was total and horribly reminiscent of France, and it was just as well that we reached Tebour Souk when we did, in the last of the light, for the Me. 109s. patrolled all the roads of the battle area and could do as they liked unopposed.

It was still raining on Christmas Day when we moved further

forward into the hills in the central zone beyond El Aroussa. Here we were summoned by Nelson Russell, who greeted Pat and me by saying that he wished us a merry Christmas next year.

The fact of me, merely a company commander, being summoned by the brigadier, is an indication of the slender resources of our miniature army. Nelson soon explained that in fact our individual companies would have to behave as independent battle groups in the vast area around us, and simply contain the opposition by a show of strength even if there was nothing to back it.

So D Company began its campaign on its own, with a free hand to make the maximum nuisance of itself.

We were slung in to the arena at Goubellat. This section in the middle was then vacant and nothing was known of the nearby opposition. The village signpost indicated fifty or so kilometres to Tunis.

I went ahead with my shadow and bodyguard Fusilier Clanachan, Nick and several other light-fingered gentry, leaving Hugh to bring up the rest of the company when we thought it wise to do so. Afterwards I realised my rashness and knew that I ought to have come with an escort capable of fighting, when the entire district was free to the enemy. Peaceful, and ominously quiet, it was all too deceptive. There was not a breath of wind and the silence was absolute.

On arrival I was greeted by my cousin Bill Bedford, one of 6th Armoured's artillery commanders – Bill was C.O. of the Ayrshire Yeomanry. He was picking his way around that unpleasant village more by way of reconnaissance for the general, but also to fix up a few O.Ps. Some of his guns were tucked away in the hills behind, otherwise he was entirely on his own. We still had much to learn, and had our opponents been enterprising they might have made interesting bags just then.

I did not like Goubellat and think that it was probably haunted. This of course was Hannibal's famous battleground. Ideal for his elephants, it was also ideal for Von Arnim's tanks, and it was probably equally desirable for Scipio to put an end to that ancient disrupter as it was for us to deal with his successor.

I found our troops to be edgy and oppressed by the atmosphere of the place, and as it was too large for us to hold in safety at night we stood off into a very large nearby farm.

For a space all was peace, though we poked forward eastwards across the Goubellat plain during the next night or two without finding a sign of human activity, enemy or otherwise. During the daytime we just lay up in the buildings out of sight and silent, and studied the vast rolling plain around us. There was enough cover on our front to have hidden an enemy division just in the middle distance, and in the background there was a long series of rolling ridges on the farther side of the plain. These were the effective limits of our range of vision. It would be nice to know who was the other side of them.

On 27 December I noticed through my glasses some activity on those low hills, perhaps two miles off across the plain. Further study revealed a number of the opposition having breakfast, apparently oblivious to all aspects of security. Perhaps they were new boys too. A number were reclining and obviously enjoying the morning sunshine – and there were several tents. They even had a fire going, with the smoke spiralling upwards in to the damp morning air. All this was a long way below the usual German standards and, from our point of view, almost too good to be true. I should hate to think that they saw anything of us, while we lay up there watching and waiting.

That evening I sent Chug out with instructions to find out what he could about the opposition on those ridges, and to create the maximum furore when he had done so. He took Corporal Rogan with two of his men and spent most of the night out, reappearing cheerfully with the dawn, having apparently reached his target – or, at least, *a* target. This in itself was quite a feat of night navigation, though he failed to locate the enemy before colliding with them. This misfortune brought to an end any prospect of the quiet reconnaissance that we needed.

However the opposition was not alert and farce followed. Chug, pushing on through the night with misguided enthusiasm, tripped over a bivouac tent in the darkness and fell on top of its outraged occupants. He said afterwards that you would not have believed anyone could have made so much noise, and that the man had positively bellowed, but as the unfortunate wretch probably had Chug's knee in his midriff as well as having a tommy gun dropped on him, he had every reason for affront. Disentangling himself and getting to his feet, Chug picked up the weapon and without further ado discharged it into the struggling mass under the canvas. He then retreated hurriedly into the night thinking it inadvisable to take matters further.

Rogan, and the others just behind Chug, had already come to the same conclusion, and ran back a hundred yards or so where they waited for him. It was in fact some time before they found each other again, and the incident was a vivid little illustration of the problems of linking up in the dark after a night action.

Really it was not a very bright idea, although it perhaps served Nelson's policy. It was a pretty mad act sending our valuable people two miles across terrain like that without a clear military purpose. Admittedly Chug probably killed a couple of the enemy but we soon found that they could do this kind of thing too.

The next night, 28 December, the opposition paid us a return call, and got mixed up with our signallers under Sergeant Duffy. There was a brief exchange and two or three stick grenades landed in their midst, but no one was hurt – only the signallers' feelings who thought that it was somebody else's job to defend them at night. However there was more to it than that. In spite of our precautions the Germans knew where we were and had come into us undetected.

On the night of the 29th Nick Jefferies took out one of his sections. We had noticed signs of activity across the plain and correctly deduced that some devilment was afoot. Nick was not exactly a tolerant character and soon got fed up with his soldiers when they annoyed him. This they did that night, so he packed them off home thinking it safer on his own. He said afterwards that they made far too much noise anyway. Going on, Nick discovered a party of two or three dozen Germans busy putting down a minefield. He lay up and watched them for a while with considerable interest; then, noticing their distraction over their absorbing task, which only a Hun could appreciate, Nick sidled quietly into the vicinity. They were making a fair amount of noise anyway.

Eventually their gefreiter decided to pack the party up, collected his men and set off home. Nick joined in behind, and being able to speak perfect German addressed himself to the rear file, having first pressed his pistol into the man's back. The German obligingly stopped while the rest of his team disappeared into the night. Nick thereupon brought his new-found friend back to us without further trouble, and thus provided the Irish Brigade with the first identification of the people we were competing with.

Nick that night set a standard that was difficult for others to live up to. However as he already had a shrewd idea of the days that were left to him he did not really mind what he did.

By now Pat Scott did not care for our being down by Goubellat. He thought that we had drawn too much attention to ourselves and that it was only a matter of time before the Germans realised our weakness there. They only needed to send in a few tanks, and they could have cut us out with the greatest of ease. They had had a lot of men out that night, and were still lying up there in those folds in front of us. In fact we already knew from Nick's prisoner that a show of strength was imminent. Our only safe course of action at that time was to stay mobile so that our embryo defences offered no fixed target to our opponents.

Pat realised this and acted immediately after spending what remained of the night talking to Nick and his prisoner. The German talked freely and fully, leaving Pat in no doubt at least of the numbers and whereabouts of his friends.

The following morning we put on quite a convincing display, Pat having forestalled the enemy by sending the whole of my company out across those rolling plains to see what we could sweep up. James Dunnill and Desmond were out too with B Company, similarly engaged. We had not gone far when we encountered the enemy, scattered about over a fairly wide front, but after a shot or two they raced off without disputing matters. These however were pickets, and judging by the speed of their flight we had surprised them.

We followed up the pickets perhaps less than judiciously and soon found that their brothers were dug in behind them and ready to fight. We came under cross fire from several of their machine guns, and our men of D Company – those who were new to it – at last experienced the vicious whip-crack of enemy bullets, realising how intensely personal war becomes when you know that you are the target.

We lost two of our men immediately ; Fusilier Roach who was

hit in the groin and died in a few minutes, and Corporal McCann who was hit in the shoulder, but was able to walk in.

B Company also lost a few of their men.

D Company on this occasion did not have to be told to take cover, and in a few minutes our own sections were edging forward and firing back. This they did to good effect, and some of our opponents picked up their traps and took to their heels. I know of no sensation so exhilarating as the sight of a flying enemy, and even these handfuls running like hares in front of us stirred those innate feelings of triumph, magical to all soldiers. It was only the briefest fire fight but our fusiliers knew they had won it.

The Germans were stupid here, and perhaps were green like some of us. Had they held their fire until we were close in on to them matters could have worn a very different look.

None the less the action, known facetiously in our regiment as the Battle of the Mosques, entirely altered the thoughts of the men of D Company. War was no longer an abstract matter. The zip of bullets around them cured them of all frivolity thereafter, and the realisation dawned that those nasty people in front had actually tried to kill them. Indeed had done so with one of our number, with whom they had breakfasted that morning. But they also knew what they could do themselves.

After a while the whole of the enemy team, about a company strong, withdrew and went back a full mile into their own hills, followed all the way by the shells of Bill Bedford's guns. The Germans also had their losses that day, and I noticed their stretcher bearers at work.

This was the end of our private war for the time being. Pat was now able to concentrate the battalion for the first time and accordingly withdrew us to the hills to the west. I was much relieved. During the last few days I knew that German reaction to our recent probing was inevitable, and that it could not have been long delayed. Also that when it came it would be total. Here in the hills we were safe – at least from the German tanks. Everyone was happier and, leaving Goubellat, we left gloom behind us too.

Before we left we buried Roach in the cemetery, learning in the process that circumspection, even in this, was necessary. Our opponents, noticing the activity, started to range upon us, and before the brief committal was over they had sent a dozen or so shells in and around us. Thereafter we did such things at night, when we could pay our last respects to our friends without the indignities of diving for cover in the process.

Hugh Holmes left us here. He was far too valuable to be risked in the squalid adventures of D Company. The poor chap was stolen from us by G.H.Q., but there were compensations thereafter as I found it most useful having this friend at court. Two and a half years later, across the turgid scene of war and a world away, he connived at, and assisted at, my marriage to one of the charming Wrens who beguiled him in Alexandria.

4

Come Wind and Weather

SAFELY INSTALLED IN our mountain redoubt I wrote home, "Life this last week has been a definite improvement . . . and by dint of digging we have made ourselves almost rainproof. Succeeded in getting most of our clothes washed this last day or two and everyone bathed biscuit-tin method, so our morale is high . . . I fear we were quite wonderfully dirty owing to lack of water . . . but we managed to shave daily.

"I have got a most comfortable dug-out, complete with my Lilo. We find it is only the simple things in life that matter here. Sleep, feeding, and remaining dry; and achieving that, everything is rosy. The dawns here have to be seen to be believed – a vivid orange glow. Our pipers are just starting to play . . . they sound rather good in these hills."

Our life in the open, in midwinter in the Tunisian mountains, was taxing in some respects, and the foul weather was an uncomfortable background to our adventures. This period was on the whole wet, and the storms when they came had the vicious element of Highland sleet, sometimes continuing on and off for days. For much of the time in January we were either soaked or gradually drying off in the aftermath of these spells, usually being blown dry in the high winds that seemed to follow them. Mostly however we were damp enough, and one's state of mind largely revolved around whether the night ahead looked like being a dry one or not.

There were other points besides that of comfort on these black wet nights with their low visibility. Then the tension was higher, and the need for alertness paramount. But there was relief too, even relaxation, when the clouds went by and the stars came out. Tunisian nights could have their attractions. Those were the times when our soldiers disclosed their innermost thoughts – and I think now of the endless low-key conversations with our N.C.Os. and sentries as the long hours passed by.

We slept when we could in the daytime, just lying up in our dug-outs, or on the hillside beside them when they were flooded; this tended to happen when cover was non-existent, and drainage operations often achieved nothing save to turn the thing in to a torrent and half drown the chap next to you.

The Tunisian mud had powers of adherence that I have never found elsewhere. A witch's brew of its own, the grey clay soil disintegrated rapidly when wet into a composition like glue mixed with baking powder, and it paralysed all movement. Furthermore only a half hour of rain was needed to achieve this devilish result. Under these conditions not even tracked vehicles could move over the land, and it was hard enough for our men on their feet.

We take the green grass of our country far too much for granted, and only the mud bath conditions of a land like Tunisia can teach one a true appreciation of our own park-like islands.

Vehicles and even tanks were lost to the enemy before the year had ended, simply through being bogged at the wrong moment, and no hand of man saved our armoured regiments in December when the storms came before their committal to battle. A few hours later, or at the most a day, and we would have handed victory to the enemy as a Christmas present with an armoured division complete. They would have been bogged to a tank, to quote Nelson's sober reflections. Never public knowledge how near a miss it had been, our commanders knew all too well, and a different turn with the weather could have ended in the virtual destruction of our army. There were three of our Grant tanks bogged in the German lines at Bou Arada in the first engagement in January, and they are no doubt there still. Horrible things, with their 75mm. cannon that could only fire to starboard. They were no loss – but the lesson remained.

As for D Company, after any activity under these conditions, we looked as though we had been dipped in French chalk.

Our men took everything for granted as usual. Extraordinarily well fed, they lacked for nothing save comfort. The brigade staff, our quartermasters and drivers, had the worst of this phase, as they so often did in the future. Water, rations and ammunition all found their way to us at night, but scarcely ever on wheels beyond our battalion H.Q. Thereafter everything had to be humped by hand, sometimes a couple of miles or more.

Mostly in this campaign we lived off the famous compo pack, which I think to be one of the most inspired rations ever served up to the British infantry. It lacked nothing, though all of it was canned save for the hard biscuit and the tea. Bread there was none, but I cannot say that we missed it.

In a letter to father I said, "Our rations are really excellent. All tinned of course and include bacon, sausage, cheese, butter, biscuits, tea mixture, puddings, and things like steak, Irish stew, Maconachie and many other delicacies, so we don't starve."

However the days were to come when we no longer cared about food. When committed to battle our men for the most part ate nothing. I certainly never did, beyond perhaps a nibble of chocolate once in a while. We simply kept going on rum. Realising this our Q.Ms., with the active connivance of the C.Os., and indeed of our brigade H.Q., went to enormous pains to indent, borrow, seize or steal immense quantities of the stuff. Eventually it became unthinkable to go into action without it. Rum, and morphia to silence our wounded.

Our C.Q.M.S. was Colour Sergeant David Bartlett. Dave was an adept scrounger, brought up,as it were, in the tradition since his happy far off days as mess corporal in Guernsey. He never lost an opportunity of producing hot, and sometimes illicit food for his company, often in improbable circumstances. As time passed this became both a custom and a point of honour with our Q. staff throughout the brigade in the aftermath of battle, and at all other times when our warriors were capable of eating.

David was materially assisted by a red-headed hero from Fermanagh. Fusilier Strainger, sometime corporal, was one of our company cooks. Promotion with Strainger could be said to lack permanency, for though he feared no enemy the same could be said of his own side too, and there were occasional disciplinary lapses. Mostly these incidents involved violent treatment of people who incurred his displeasure. If they occurred within the company I never heard about them, but unfortunately he had a well developed contempt for other regiments, which occasionally led to bothers if he got excited. I was very fond of him and he never failed us in battle. He was also an admirable cook when not otherwise diverted.

My two private acolytes at this time were Bill Price my batman, a Sassenach like myself from the Midlands, and Fusilier Clanachan, later corporal, my orderly and much else, who scarcely ever left my side. He also was from Fermanagh.

Another character of distinction was Quinlan, my driver. Fusilier Quinlan was from Dublin, and being brought up in the best Irish tradition he was a rebel until joining the Faughs. Now he was a devoted servant of the king. The relationship between a company commander and his driver can become peculiarly personal. Often one sat through the long hours of the night with him, when no secrets are hid, and I think I eventually captured his affection when discussing the sad tale of Parnell and Kitty O'Shea, who he fervently admired.

Then there was Fusilier Jack Birch – one of our stretcher bearers, who looked like Old Bill and showed a dogged indifference to all the circumstances around him, however good they might be, or bad. He too was destined for unsought fame.

A few nights later we lost Chug Sutcliffe. Chug, like Stonewall Jackson at Chancellorville, died from the fire of his own pickets in a tense situation with the enemy nearby. It was a hazard inseparable from war and only hard experience taught us how to avoid these things. Of course one's standing posts, alert always to warn us, presented extreme danger to their own nocturnal visitors as well as to the enemy. Circumspection was ever necessary when approaching them, and usually it was only safe to identify oneself to them by careful pre-arrangement, and from dead ground. All this was soon to become second nature, but I alone could have saved Chug had I had the foresight to warn him.

We lost two more of our men in a patrol clash later that night – Barry and Maxwell, both of Chug's platoon.

PLATE I

Grandstand Hill. The forward posts and O.P. Opposite, Two Tree Hill is prominent against the sky, though minus its trees.

PLATE 2

Grandstand Hill, southern end. Point 286 lies in the middle distance on the extreme right of picture and Two Tree Hill is the high feature on the left.

Tragedies of this kind were extremely rare in the Irish Brigade, and I think that our record in this respect attests the standard of discipline which held our people together. A year later, in other mountains, one of my posts shot and killed every man of an American signal detachment who wandered in to them in the depths of the night without warning or expectation. Perturbed I went along the next morning to see their regimental commander and to express my regrets. With typical American generosity he greeted me affectionately, and finished by remarking, "Think nothing of it, brother, it happens every night."

None the less, our attitude was a different one, and with us these things were personal.

The following night, 6 January, I sent Douglas Walsh out with a view to apprehending any German activity on the north-south road over the plain at the back of the Mosque ridge, and attacking any suitable targets.

Douglas took Robbie with him, Lance Corporal Johnson, Smith 05, and several others, and they found their way to the road all right, but not a sign of activity when they got there. They lay up there all night, and a particularly icy one too, when no sensible German would think of venturing for pleasure. The trouble started when they were due to return, and they found themselves so frozen up that some of the warriors were fuddled. They could hardly move themselves, and with numbed fingers and even number wits one hesitates to think what might have happened if they had had to use their weapons hurriedly.

In the ordinary way it should have taken Douglas less than an hour to cover the two miles back home, but in fact he returned in the daylight after travelling ten miles at least and stirring all of us to extreme apprehension – feelings which were fully shared by his frozen and demoralised posse, and not without reason.

Feeling that the patrol was casting along in a vast circle and apparently heading ever deeper in to enemy territory, Robbie tactfully took a look at Douglas's compass. After doing so he mentioned to his commander the inadvisability of taking bearings on the thing when resting it on a tommy gun, and after eliminating that variable they did at last head for home instead of Tunis.

They finally finished up in collision with an American flak unit five miles north of our sector, and only Robbie's extreme instinct for safety prevented them being shot down by the American sentries.

It was not one of our best nights.

In that first week of January, though we did not then appreciate the point, we were as children playing with fire.

The Germans had now landed the main components of four high grade divisions in the country, in addition to the parachute regiments, and on 9 December the whole were embodied under the title of the 5th Panzer Army, or P3 AOK 5, to use the German designation. Nehring was superseded, apparently being of insufficient rank by German standards for the command of an army. He was succeeded by Generaloberst Jürgen von Arnim, but considering Walther Nehring's brief but impressive record in that critical first month, and his known capacity and previous performance in the Africa Corps, the allies may have been fortunate in the change.

On our sector we had the privilege of facing the 10th Panzer Division, Koch's 5th Para Regiment and the Stürmregiment of the Hermann Göring Division, usually known as the J.R.H.G., and then attached to the 10th Panzers. This latter regiment, the Jäger Regiment Hermann Göring, although one of the best units in the theatre, had the dubious advantage of being under the control, or veto, of the Reichmarshal, a restraint which evidently applied to Luftwaffe troops.

I cannot think why these people did not obliterate the Irish Brigade at the outset. The all-protecting weather may have had something to do with it, but had they used their opportunities at the turn of the year to take a swipe at us instead of casting about for territory, our first battle could well have been our last one.

However in the second week of the new year, feeling their strength, the enemy thrust south and then south-west, thinking to unhook us at a sensitive point where our southern flank linked up with the French zone.

About fifteen miles to the south of us was the little town of Bou Arada, then scarcely in the war zone. This part of the sector until now had not attracted the interest of either side, and the only military presence was a half battalion of French riflemen who occupied the town itself. But the importance of the locality was undeniable due to the hill bastions which surrounded it, and which dominated the westward passes on our southern flank.

It is not suprising that the area attracted the attention of the Germans as it offered the prospect of turning the whole of the First Army front in Tunisia, and after their first probe at so sensitive a spot it became of absorbing interest to both sides for the rest of the campaign.

In the meantime the 6th Armoured Division was responsible for our southern front, and as a precaution the division kept a daily picket and a scout car on the top of an obscure little mound a few miles north-east of the town. This insignificant feature was called Two Tree Hill. It was destined for fame and would never be forgotten by those who knew it.

Two Tree Hill owed its tactical importance to being higher than its neighbours. Overlooking the flat ground northwards and eastwards it provided both a defensive outwork as well as an observation post that could see to the coast. In German hands it would provide a like service in the opposite direction. The hill itself, like the other small features near it, was a blighted spot, steep sided and covered in small rocks and scree, and was virtually unapproachable without the goodwill of the residents.

The picket were breakfasting one morning in their O.P. on the top of the hill, their scout cars a short way below, when they noticed in the half light of dawn a column of vehicles coming in fast from the east. Our men waited upon events evidently spellbound, while the column approached, never apparently once considering until far too late that the passengers could be unfriendly. Finally the column came to a halt below them, parking, with their Teutonic sense of proper order, in the immediate vicinity of the scout cars. The picket had tarried too long but they had the fascinating experience of watching a German battalion de-bussing by numbers in front of them. Others followed. Oberstleutnant Walter Koch had arrived.

Lacking imagination, or perhaps being able to consider only one thing at a time while the unteroffiziers were dressing the ranks, the Jägers failed to react with their usual speed. Our men ran for it and were in and away down that muddy scree-strewn track before their dumbfounded visitors had time to turn nasty.

None the less this was the start of our troubles, for the enemy, having once seized Two Tree Hill, soon regarded the feature as the south-west cornerstone of their whole defence system ; thus the rock that the builders neglected. Our people soon came to the same conclusion, and wanted it back immediately.

However at that time the Germans had the initiative and the advantage, and they pushed on from Two Tree Hill with a view to seizing the whole of the high ground round Bou Arada, pinching out the town in the process.

This considerable disturbance was immediately to the south on the Irish Brigade sector, but on 11 January Nelson ordered the London Irish to carry out a sweep across the southern end of the Goubellat plain, which was the adjoining territory. This they did without serious engagement, but matters were very different on the Bou Arada front. Here the 6th Armoured Division sent in the Rifle Brigade with the object of disinfesting the area and recapturing Two Tree Hill. They did not succeed and accordingly the Inniskillings were sent round there, then ourselves, and finally the whole resources of the Irish Brigade were required. Even then we could do no more than stabilise the sector, which was very near to collapsing.

The enemy were in fact all over the high ground north of Bou Arada, and across the north-south road from there to our late home of Goubellat. They certainly could not be allowed to stay in secure possession of a district which unhinged the entire allied line, and had the Germans been left to it they could have curled up the whole front from the bottom end upwards. Our situation had suddenly become one of extreme hazard, deliberately created by Von Arnim and no doubt in accordance with the Führer's initial appreciation.

I do not think that our army realised at the time just how well the Rifle Brigade had carried out their task. They were only a battalion, the 10th Rifle Brigade, and they were contending with a whole regiment of Jägers, though the latter were effectively dispersed over a large area of broken country. However the riflemen drove them out of most of their forward posts before they were fully established, and chased them back to the east of the Goubellat road. Here the riflemen were badly cut up in the approaches to Two Tree Hill and could go no further.

We were on our way to the area the following day, Tuesday 12 January, Pat Scott taking C and D Companies with him only. Before we started Peter Murphy came over and asked me what had happened to cause this insult to A Company, who by title and tradition had the first right to enter the battle. I told Peter not to be such a fire-eater, and that my reading of the situation was that the time would come for all of us and mighty soon too, when he would have all the fighting that he was ever likely to want.

We called in at brigade headquarters on route, going round the back way via El Aroussa. There we had lunch with Nelson, and my principal recollection of his briefing was the assumption that the enemy forces in front of us were of small account. In the afterlight I do not believe that at that time our army had the slightest idea of the opposition in front of us on that sector. The whole thing had blown up in the last two or three days, and we neither read the signs nor measured up what we were contending with. No attempt was made to do so, and I consider now that we were reacting blindly. Nelson went on to say that the enemy had made a nuisance of themselves by occupying several small hills which were tactically important to us, and he fully expected that the Irish Brigade would eject these people without any particular difficulty. He then continued with the details.

Nelson was of course simply carrying out his orders based on his own briefing at that time, but he revised his opinions drastically a day or two later as soon as he learned the true facts.

A few hours later we found ourselves on a low ridge in the centre of the disputed area. This was Grandstand Hill, lying immediately east of the Bou Arada-Goubellat road, and tactically of the highest importance because of that fact. It had just been recaptured by the Rifle Brigade and was the farthest point secured and held in their previous day's counter attack.

D Company came on to the feature in a thunderstorm that evening and took it over, releasing the Inniskillings who had followed up the Rifle Brigade and who were earmarked for the star part the following morning. For the time being we shared the feature with one of the Rifle Brigade companies, while C Company acted as backstop on the ridge behind us on the other side of the road. I was not exactly happy as we had lost 17 Platoon on the way ; I later discovered that they had broken down, and I daresay Douglas and his men had a tense few hours on their own in that desolate region. However they reappeared safely and cheerfully the following morning.

That night of our arrival I went back to the Rifle Brigade headquarters where we were briefed for our respective parts in the next day's events. The riflemen mentioned that they had my cousin Ted there in the R.A.P. and would I like to see him? Ted Bedford's company of 10 Rifle Brigade had taken a leading part in the previous day's adventures, and when they were pinned down in the last stages of that attack on Two Tree Hill one of Koch's marksmen had shot him through the neck.

Ted was prostrate but cheerful, and he had much to say about his experiences during that grim and bloody little battle. At least I could give a first-hand account to Aunt Eva as to the state of her son, but if others had listened to what Ted and his brother officers had said that night, and heeded it, the series of tragedies ahead of us might have ended differently.

Our people were behind the event and one of the factors may well have been the age old problem of communication – of ensuring that accurate information from those on the spot, and all the implication of it, actually reached the ears of our commanders at the highest level.

However Pat Scott with his usual candour remarked that "they jolly well knew the facts all right but couldn't get the message over to the old man",* which is perhaps another way of saying the same thing. Whatever the reason, we underestimated our enemy just then, and unfortunately persisted in the error.

The following day at 5 a.m. the Inniskillings were sent in to eliminate the opposition, then two or three times their own strength. By any standards it was an ill-considered action for an objective that was a long way short of being vital. The battle was not laid on with the careful pre-planning of later times, and there was never the remotest chance of success. We know this now but

*The Army Commander. General Sir Kenneth Anderson.

we were also pretty sure of the likely result at the time, in view of what the Rifle Brigade had told us. There was a feeling of impulsive recklessness about this attack and that the known facts were being ignored not only at army level but at all levels, for reasons that I have never fathomed.

At that stage it was vital to keep our own forces intact to resist our rapidly growing enemy, but this was simply squandering. Worse was to come.

After fighting all morning the Inniskillings never even reached the forward slopes of their objective. It had rained heavily for most of the night and they had to slough on under a hail of fire from both front and flanks. The troop of Grant tanks that accompanied them never got near the place before getting bogged, and the poor traverse of their casemated 75 mm. cannon prevented any effective close support. The unfortunate troop commander came back to commiserate afterwards – on foot.

The poor Skins held on as best they could during the afternoon, and withdrew through us at dusk, having lost a hundred of their men and some of their best officers. We, D Company, were now left to contain the horde opposite, and as partners we had Dick Fyffe and his company of the 10th Rifle Brigade. Here we sat on our ugly ridge by the Goubellat road. Famous under its new-christened title of "Grandstand Hill" it was in fact just that, with Two Tree Hill a mile opposite and a horrible arena between us.

All was peace for twenty-four hours while both sides thought out their next moves.

We were shelled intermittently during the afternoon but, safely dug in by then, there were no casualties, unless one includes Nicolas. Nick had a splinter through an ear. Picturesquely bloody I told him he was a stupid ass and that it was his own fault. He never hurried under fire and usually scorned cover. Nick's sense of dignity was distinctly warped.

Bill Bedford came in to see us later, having been busy registering the defensive fire tasks of his guns. Bill at least had no illusions about the next likely train of events. He explained his arrangements and stayed to have tea with us. It was comforting to know that his fire curtain was on tap – and it would prove decisive in the next act in the drama.

I then sent Nick out at nightfall with one of his sections, to see who was around and to upset similar action by our opponents. He exceeded his orders as usual.

Penetrating to the top of Two Tree Hill itself, which a whole regiment had failed to reach the previous day, Nicolas tossed several grenades into the dug-outs that he found on the top, and then withdrew as a squall of fire went over his head. The half dozen men with him vanished, and that was the last that Nick or anyone else saw of them in this world, other than the one or two who survived in enemy hands. Nick came back on his own, quite unperturbed and snorting with rage at his men's conduct. He said he preferred to go out alone in future. He may have been right in view of the kind of things he did. No soldier ever came up to the standards that Nick required.

The following morning as the stark outline of the ridges appeared against that first glow of the dawn, we noticed that something had happened – that tantalising hill was somehow different. Then the penny dropped. Our humourless adversaries had cut down the two trees, realising their significance. But I suppose they could hardly be expected to regard Nicolas' visit as a joke.

As for Pat Scott, he took one look and only made one remark – "Spiteful", he said.

5

Koch

KOCH'S PARATROOPERS HAD flown in to Tunisia in mid-November, and his soldiers apparently expected to be out of the place a month later, on the basis that their function was only to cure local disturbances, as indeed they had done in Crete and elsewhere.

There seems to have been a feeling that they were being misused when they found that they were being left in the country and, worse still, incorporated with other troops. Such treatment upset them due to the social affront as much as for purely military reasons. In this respect it has sometimes been said that the British army tended to be class conscious, but if this was true we were non-starters in comparison with the German Wehrmacht – that is if Koch's 5th Parachute Regiment was in any way typical.

The German force on our front at Bou Arada was of exceptional quality and the Irish Brigade could rightly have regarded their presence as complimentary. But Koch's soldiers did not feel like this. When their recently promoted regimental commander moved his men into the district they were attached to the 10th Panzer Division, which already included Hermann Göring's Jägers, and these pet mountain troops of the Reich Marshal had feelings of exclusiveness fully the equal of the paras, who declined to recognise them. As the Jägers did not recognise anybody else either, it must have made life trying for their commander.

These were the two regiments who were our principal opponents in the weeks to come, and as time passed we came to have a considerable professional regard and respect for them. Dangerous as enemies they fought a clean war, and pleasantries were passed whenever the circumstances permitted.

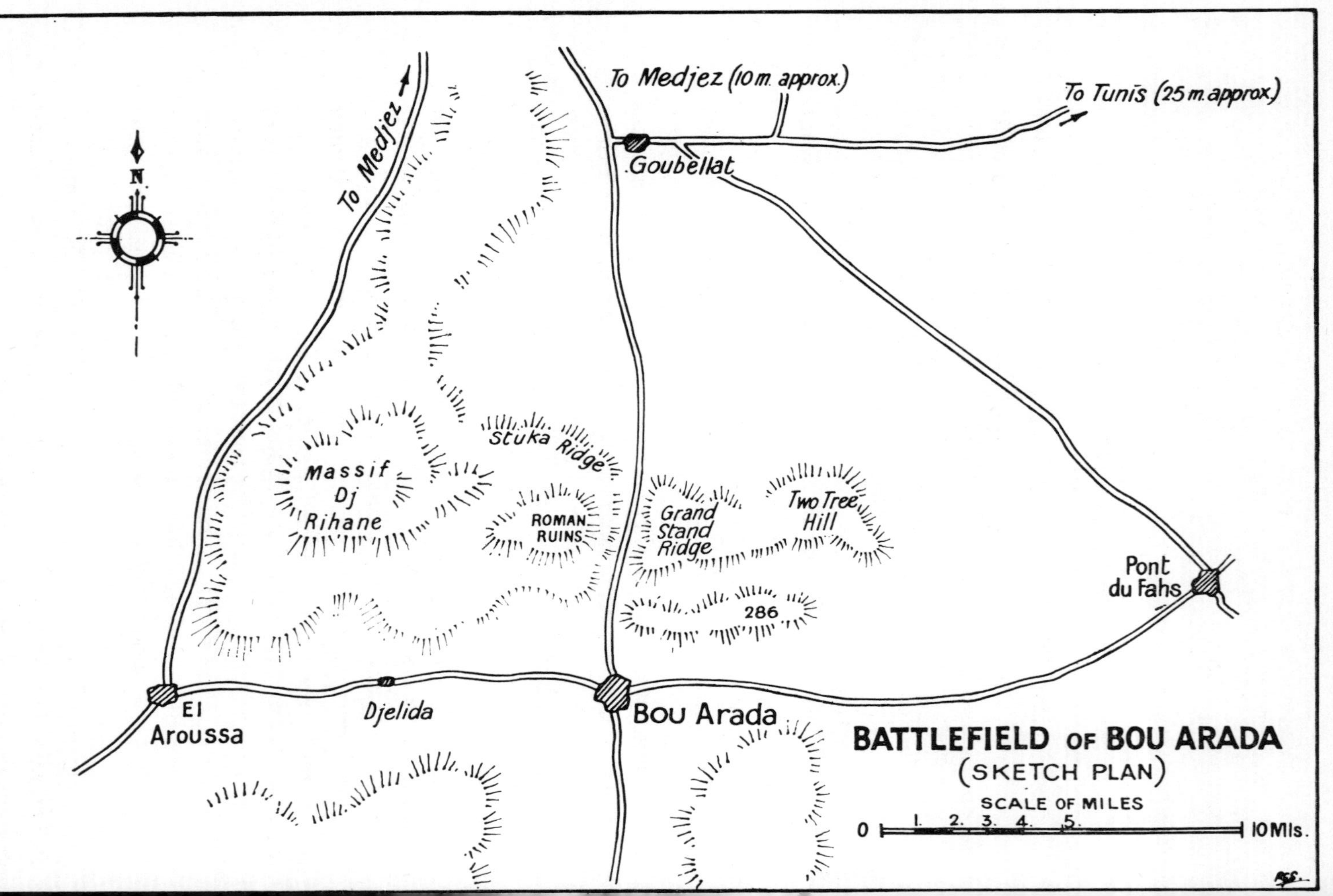
To Medjez (10 m. approx.)
To Tunis (25 m. approx.)
To Medjez
N
Goubellat
Stuka Ridge
Massif Dj Rihane
ROMAN RUINS
Grand Stand Ridge
Two Tree Hill
286
Pont du Fahs
El Aroussa
Djelida
Bou Arada
BATTLEFIELD OF BOU ARADA
(SKETCH PLAN)
SCALE OF MILES
0 1. 2. 3. 4. 5. 10 Mls.

Koch was quite a person. Oberstleutnant Walter Koch had been decorated with the Ritter Kreuz in 1940 for his performance in storming the barrier fortress of Eban Emael when he commanded the Stürm battalion of the 5th Paras as a hauptmann. Taking them through the whole of the Battle of France, he had commanded his regiment ever since. Koch and his men had therefore been together for a long time and, dropping in the third wave at Malême in Crete, they had not suffered the casualties which decimated the rest of the German forces in that classic airborne attack.

It would hardly have been possible to find a more professional force anywhere in the German army at that time, and Obergefreiter Heinz Preussner has made it quite clear what they thought of themselves. They regarded all other troops with contempt – that is the French and Americans, and their feeling for the rest of the German army could only be described as one of patronising toleration. Heinz said that there were reservations about the British, but he may just have been trying to be polite. However he did mention that the oberst was considered to have done exceptionally well in his performance against us, so the respect was apparently mutual.

The paras had been moving about a bit up to this stage, but the force now on our front at Bou Arada, covering the German sector south of Medjez from Goubellat to Pont du Fahs, consisted of the three battalions of Oberst Koch's own regiment, the first and third battalions of the Jäger Regiment Hermann Göring (J.R.H.G.), the second battalion apparently still being in transit, and various other lesser fry added from time to time. They had the whole of the rest of the 10th Panzer Division to back them, which at the time was at full strength. The division included the 7th Panzer Regiment of tanks, two other infantry regiments, the 69th and 86th, the A4 Infantry Battalion, one artillery regiment, and a battalion of armoured infantry, Panzerjägers, who performed the same role as the 10th Rifle Brigade in our own armoured division. Apart from some restrictions in artillery ammunition the division seems to have lacked for nothing.

The 10th Panzer Division could not be said to be a lucky one, though it left its mark in history. Its commander was Generalleutnant Wolfgang Fischer, who was in his last month of eventful and not altogether successful life before he went up on one of his own mines with his chief of staff beside him. This was sad as both men were then enjoying that capricious favour sometimes found in Hitler's Wehrmacht – but seldom for long. Both had been honoured after their initial victories in the bridge-head battles in November, Fischer with the Oak Leaves, the Eichenlaub, and Oberstleutnant Bürker, his assistant, with the Ritter Kreuz.

The latter officer, the chief of staff, was replaced by none other than Oberstleutnant Graf von Stauffenberg, who became famous for ever in German history and extolled as a martyr for his attempt to blow up his Führer. The luckless but valiant oberst finished up in front of a firing squad. Certainly the 10th Panzers attempted great matters, but there was a tendency for them to go wrong at the last moment.

However there was one factor which we soon discovered on our front, that whatever their feelings for their higher commanders Oberstleutnant Walter Koch was respected to the point of reverence by his own paratroopers.

Our army headquarters could hardly have appreciated the threat on our front just then, and the underestimation of the quality and strength of our adversaries is quite staggering when considering it in the afterlight. With the seemingly total failure of our intelligence at this time, or the ignoring of it perhaps, there appears to have been little attempt to read the enemy's mind, and the First Army seems to have been bent on its own plans without fully considering other factors. I can conceive of no more dangerous attitude, and find it incredible in our circumstances then with so few troops in the theatre and so much to lose.

Although they failed in the end the Germans managed to surprise us completely at the outset, and the extent of that surprise is a reflection upon us.

Apparently ignoring the experience first of the Rifle Brigade and now the Inniskillings, yet another battalion assault was to be mounted, thinking that concentrated artillery would achieve the desired result this time. The new plan was put in hand at a time when we would need the whole of our strength to defend ourselves, and it was ordered for dawn on 18 January.

Pat Scott is adamant that had the attack actually happened it would probably have seen the end of the Irish Brigade, and with that brick taken out of its all too skimpy foundations the disintegration of the army would have been an inevitable sequel. If anyone has any doubts about this they only have to consider what Rommel had previously achieved with his armour in the desert, and what would have been open to the 10th Panzer Division to do when we were no longer in their path.

Sir Charles Keightley, the divisional commander, detested the plan and said so, finding that his corps commander shared his views. Pat said that in his and Sir Charles's view Brigadier Ambrose Pratt was entirely responsible for saving the army, and discussing it together afterwards they concluded that it was the nearest squeak that they ever experienced, making them cold even to think about it years later.

Brigadier Pratt was the corps artillery commander, and after discussing his part in this attack with his chief, Sir Charles Allfrey, both men came to the same conclusion as their divisional commander. Ambrose then stated that the artillery support for the battle was inadequate and that he needed more time to get additional guns in. This kind of opinion could not be gainsaid, and between the two of them they at last persuaded the army commander to a twenty-four hour postponement – and this brief delay, enemy misjudgment, or the intervention of our Divine guardians, according to how one looks at these things, combined together to kill the plan.

Nelson of course realised the position, and I knew at the time that Pat Scott recognised the venture as a pretty hazardous one from what he said to me in his briefing. Pat never tried to minimise things and I am thankful that he didn't. His intuitive sense could always be relied on, and I shall never forget the relief of both of them when we were saved from our ordeal by our adversaries.

Most of us knew instinctively that the plan of battle was a bad one, and that it would fail. However I doubt if the company officers appreciated that the whole brigade was at risk just then – or the immensity of the stakes being set down for such an indifferent jackpot.

In justice to the army commander, Sir Charles did mention to Pat that he was being much pressed from home by an impatient Winston.

The tactical aspects of actions of this kind were very unsatisfactory, and isolated assaults on strongly held positions rarely succeeded. These finger thrusts were easily engulfed from the flanks, and even if simply repelled, like the Inniskillings on the 13th, it was still pointless to lose a hundred men and one's best officers solely to capture ground – however tactically important the latter might seem to be. All that mattered was to make sure of smashing the enemy when the vital time arrived, but that could hardly be done if our infantry regiments were wrecked beforehand.

We must be thankful that the Skins failed to take those features in their attack on 13 January, for had they done so I am sure that they would have been pinched out and utterly destroyed afterwards as the 10th Panzer Division closed in upon them. We were too thin on the ground ever to have held those hills far out on our front like that, and beyond reach of support; our enterprising enemy would never have lost such a chance.

Moreover we were just about to witness a first-class example of what could happen in these circumstances, and it would never be forgotten by the Irish Brigade.

On the ground fortunately the sixth sense often comes to the rescue when extreme danger is breathing down one's neck. However it failed us on 18 January, and on this occasion salvation came not from our own efforts but from those of Generalleutnant Wolfgang Fischer and brother Koch.

Undeterred by all this stir among our chiefs, or by the Inniskillings' lost battle, the third attempt was now resolved upon, and against such a background Winston's ruminations and proddings of his army commander finally ended in Pat's reluctant orders to his mercifully unimaginative warriors in D Company. For this time we, D Company, had been selected for the lead. No doubt it was a great honour, but then tragedy always gave better opportunities for inspired acting than farce ever did. Perhaps we should have both.

As a preliminary the battered Skins returned to Grandstand, to provide a jumping-off point for our own assault. I did not like the idea much, but I thought that we had better have a look at what we were in for. We said goodbye to Dick Fyffe and his riflemen, and on the night of the 16th I went out with Nicolas.

It was quite a bright night with a moon that appeared fitfully, and one could see quite a long way. Nicolas and I covered each other forward, going along the southern and flatter side of the German positions, and passing on our way the sombre hulks of those three wrecked Grants. We discovered first a posse of the other side laying mines; then working round past Two Tree Hill itself to its lower slopes beyond we observed a number of tanks. We came across only one German who evidently mistook us for one of his own team – that is if he saw us at all. I leant against an olive tree, in its shadow, watching the man for a while and prepared to shoot, while Nick sat sketching his observations on to his note-pad.

The following day was spent in uneasy preparation for battle, but we need not have worried, for our obliging enemy was doing likewise and would save us the trouble of putting our own plans in to effect. I cannot remember what they were now, though I recall being extremely interested in keeping the enemy positions under smoke for the duration. With seventy-two guns supporting us I think we would have got on to the feature somehow, but having done so, that would have been the end of the matter for us, for all time.

Some of those guns included the 17th Field Regiment, new to the 78th Division but associated thereafter with the Irish Brigade until the end of Hitler.

The 17th Field were late, like the Faughs themselves, and had only reached Bou Arada that very day, having been torpedoed in the last days of their voyage to North Africa. Beached at Bougie, there had been unloading and ferrying problems, not improved by the German dive bombers becoming interested in them.

On the late night of Sunday 17 January the 17th Field Regiment tucked themselves and their guns into position on the northern outskirts of Bou Arada, astride the road leading to Goubellat, and they could hardly have chosen any place on the whole German perimeter in Tunisia with greater significance, or timed it more auspiciously. However their presence just then could hardly be said to be a coincidence, and perhaps it was merely another entry to chalk up to Ambrose Pratt and his far-sighted corps commander.

While these important matters were in train D Company had taken up positions on a feature which became notorious as Stuka Ridge, a title which was fully earned in the days immediately ahead of us. It was a mile-long straggly feature with little growing on it save spiky scrub which hid nothing, and it was scored by shallow fissures and runners descending the steep northern face. These also provided negligible cover until improved by digging. The surface of the ridge was mostly ground-up scree-like rock chippings.

Half a mile behind us on the ridge was the French farm steading which gave its name to the ridge, and was a principal source of interest to the opposing airmen. Nelson, in a fit of absent-mindedness, selected the place initially for his tactical headquarters, but soon repented and dug his people in, in less attractive places, like the rest of us.

Stuka Ridge faced north, and it covered the left flank of the Inniskillings on Grandstand. The Goubellat road ran northwards between us, and in the dips behind were Bill Bedford's guns, battalion headquarters and, dominating the whole, the vast wooded mountain mass of Djebel Rihane. Stuka Ridge was vital to the defence of Grandstand, and the loss of either feature would have cost us the other. The Germans knew this and made their battle plans accordingly.

A disturbed night followed, and then by the mercy of Allah, before the first orange glow appeared in the eastern sky, and before the Irish Brigade could expend yet another battalion against those sinister little hills standing there silhouetted, General Fischer took matters in to his own hands and unleashed his formidable infantry upon us.

The assault was carried out by the 1st and 3rd Jägers, three other infantry battalions of the 10th Panzer Division, and an abteilung of about three squadrons from their 7th Panzer Regiment. That is a total of five infantry battalions and two dozen or so tanks.

Part of this considerable force, and the armour, pushed on down the plain towards Bou Arada and over the lower slopes to the south of our position, but the J.R.H.G. went head-on into the Innis-

PLATE 3

Grandstand Hill. Under close view of the enemy. The slit carved through its top gave accessibility to the forward posts in daylight.

PLATE 4
Djebel Rihane from reverse of Grandstand, facing west. Shows the Irish Brigade defensive zone in depth, and gun positions.

killings on Grandstand. By the time it was light on that Monday morning of 18 January the Jägers were at close grips with the Skins. The whole lot of us were under intense shellfire interspersed with the shrieking howl of the Spandau machine guns, which appeared to be coming from all over the Inniskilling positions as well as from between us.

It soon became obvious that the enemy had seized at least a part of their objective and were between us and the Skins.

After a while, when it became possible to see anything, it seemed that the enemy had penetrated on to the northern end of the ridge of Grandstand, and were busily engaged in tossing grenades down on an Inniskilling platoon beneath them. We let rip at them with our machine guns, but without much effect, as they crawled among the rocks. I pushed 16 Platoon forward a few hundred yards to close up the gap between us and the Skins, and there we were stuck for the time being – with a number of determined Jägers between us who could certainly go no further, but nor for that matter could we.

Bill Bedford had the whole of his regiment on the Irish Brigade front, and with the rest of the division's guns within reach the effect of the artillery was decisive. After the initial impact, like Porsena of old, it was a case of "those behind cried forward and those before cried back". But the gentlemen mixed up with the Inniskillings could not get back, not with the fire of seventy guns coming down behind them. However I noticed that this did not deter the German stretcher bearers.

Ordered to counter attack in the late afternoon, Peter Murphy took A Company round the right end of Grandstand, and came in on their rear covered by some of our tanks. Peter's men went in in line under a storm of fire, criss-crossing over and through them from their front and flanks.

As A Company closed, the enemy ran for it, coming under intense fire as they broke cover. Peter died in these last few moments. Typical Pete – with his piper beside him. I don't think D Company would have done it that way. Perhaps crawled in and shot them out – perhaps not. I do not know. I only do know that sending an infantry company across that open arena, under the admiring gaze of the entire teams of both protagonists, fully merited the famous French tribute on Cardigan's charge at Balaclava, "C'est magnifique, mais. . . ." "Mais" indeed. However it will live in the archives like all acts of true valour.

We also lost Mike Barstow then, Peter's second in command, who was shot through the temple and blinded. He was recovered about a mile out in no man's land twenty-four hours later, after intensive searching by our stretcher bearers. The rest of our injured men were nearer in, but Mike had wandered helplessly from the scene of the action, and the fact that he was found at all may well have been due to enemy compassion.

Our stretcher bearers for the first time had come in to contact with their opposite numbers of the German army, apparently by mutual impulse, for both needed information from the other as to the whereabouts of their men. The need for this was all too evident, for the soldiers of both sides lay scattered over a square mile of broken ground, with those of A Company intermixed with their late opponents.

There were several minutes of amicable discussion on the stricken battlefield, before they parted with mutual courtesies and expressions of esteem.

At the other end of our front an equally confused battle was fought to its conclusion when the 7th Panzers collided with the 17th Field Regiment. An open sight brawl developed immediately, which was hardly a professional start for Ian Lawrie's first battle, though we owe it to his regiment that Fischer's armoured thrust was finally halted. Expensive to both sides the German tank losses were irreplaceable, though their enterprising crews recovered most of them after nightfall.

Perhaps it does not do to dwell on the outcome had the 17th Field Regiment not plugged that gap when they did, with a few hours in hand. But for them I fancy that the Irish Brigade might have found itself surrounded before the day had ended.

The battle died down as the evening wore on, but our late opponents did not go far. They held on to the nearby ridges, but this time they were in more trouble than we were.

We had lost seven of D Company. White and Wood, both promising N.C.Os., and Haywood and Webster were dead, with three others wounded including Corporal Shields. Well dug in and carefully posted, our brother Skins this time had come off lightly. They had fought splendidly and given up nothing, but we could not forget A Company. However two dozen or more of the Jägers had surrendered to Peter's remnants, and the ground on and around Grandstand Hill was littered with German dead when the day had ended. Beyond doubt this was a defensive victory.

Vicious as ever, next morning the enemy concluded with a Stuka attack on Pat's H.Q. as their final venting of spleen. Pat had to jump for it and appeared later with a very black eye. I must say that his H.Q. was perhaps a bit obvious. I was quite worried seeing his place blotted out by those colossal explosions around it.

Generalleutnant Fischer did not pause for a minute. Following the usual German practice after rebuff he sent Walter Koch and his paratroopers probing elsewhere, and they now tried their luck in the southern part of the sector; but here lay the London Irish. Our own front suddenly quietened, but Oberstleutnant Koch, ever adept at trouble making, was not long in finding another sensitive spot.

Below and south of Grandstand there was a low profile sausage-shaped ridge which dominated our supply road from Bou Arada, the road which went on north through our positions to Goubellat. Seizing the ridge, which until then had not been defended, the oberst made a neat pass at severing our connections, though he could hardly have stayed there for long unless he dispossessed us of our other positions which overlooked it, beginning with Grandstand.

This ridge with its infamous bloodstained high spot, Hill 286, was something that mattered and the point was a tender one, though it could hardly have been said to be vital. Koch could not sit on our end of the thing anyway without our goodwill, and unless he could do that it was impossible for him to deny us the road once darkness had fallen. As for the road, we had never used it in daylight without extreme hazard as it was under view from the other enemy positions.

Koch's occupancy was no doubt designed to exasperate, but the correct way of dealing with the nuisance was not immediately obvious.

The matter was apparently resolved at army level most certainly wrongly, and Nelson was ordered to seize the feature and extirpate the intruders. Nelson I believe objected so extremely that the corps commander either came down, or was sent down, personally to enforce the order. That being so, poor Sir Charles would have needed no further convincing that the man on the spot was worth heeding – though knowing Nelson he knew that already but merely had to carry out his orders like the rest of us.

Nelson's objections were simply that Hill 286 was untenable by either side, being under the close domination of both, and we had got on perfectly well all this while without it.

The orders were duly carried out.

The London Irish went in to the attack the following day, with the support of the divisional artillery, and well before dusk the entire feature was in their hands in what appeared at first sight to be a straightforward operation – though their riflemen had had to fight hard enough to get it. However it soon wore the look of a trap, and no doubt Koch's men knew it was. It was also a rotten, rocky place to dig in. In fact most of the ridge was the living rock, destitute of earth, and under incessant fire from the enemy mortars our brother riflemen began to suffer serious casualties. The famous Longstop Hill was lost for exactly similar reasons. The Rifles had a very trying afternoon, but worse followed.

In the meantime Pat Scott, sensing trouble, had sent James Dunnill down there with B Company to secure the road and guard our southern flank, regardless of what might be happening on Hill 286. His and Nelson's intuition did not often fail us.

There was no delay at all before the storm burst, and the German counter attack came in like a visitation from the angels of hell complete with chariots of fire. The force and vigour of the onslaught was only matched by its audacity. True disciples of Rommel, the tank commanders rode in, sitting on the turret tops armed with Very pistols and star shells to guide them. They simply charged along the ridge from one end to the other with a solid phalanx of tanks, leaving their Jägers to pick up the bits later. Driving straight over the top of the feature in the starlight they went on, and down, and over the road itself in an ever widening torrent, and our defence dissolved into fragments before them.

The 7th Panzers were certainly showmen, and they put on a very spectacular performance, impressive even to us two ridges away, with solid streams of tracer and coloured lights flying in all directions. Moreover the German artillery was plastering the area with shell fire regardless of their tank crews charging around in it.

James Dunnill's men stood their ground, but they were gravely disorganised by the London Irish survivors of this armoured tornado. For a space they were unable to tell friend from foe in the madhouse around them. However for the most part they quietly stayed put in their posts, largely invisible, and waited for their fiendish visitors to leave them.

Our gallant brother riflemen had just too much to cope with that day – but they would repay in full in later times and on other fields.

In the meantime one of our regiments was now shattered, and it was the fault of all of us. Wolfgang Fischer was very near to having the last word, and had shown that he was no commander to trifle with. His purpose achieved, he withdrew his myrmidons – but who could say, now, that we had won the battle.

That rock-bound ridge and Point 286 that crowned it were not defensible and it was a pity that we had to ruin one of our infantry battalions to prove it. It was of course necessary to eject the enemy, but afterwards it was a place to contain by artillery in daylight and by pickets at night.

There were other lessons, among them the need for vigilance, for no precaution is any use without it. Our men had put down anti-tank mines – the standard deterrent to armoured counter attack – but unfortunately, as Pat discovered later, they had forgotten to arm them.

As for the Germans, their effort that night was a classic cavalry action, worthy of Prince Rupert himself.

6

Darkness is Absolute, Silence is Golden

THE DISTURBANCES TEMPORARILY ended, both Nelson Russell and Pat now had to take stock. Having for practical purposes lost one of our battalions owing to the calamitous losses of our riflemen, Nelson at least had to ensure that the other two regiments were made good.

Even the gallant oberst over the hill was now having to consider, with our door slammed shut in his face at Grandstand and the uneasy stalemate in the south.

For a week we were left in peace, other than for sporadic shelling from the garrison opposite and the daily visitations from Stukas.

The gaps in the Faugh ranks were all too noticeable. Nick and Douglas were my only officers in D Company, and with twenty battle casualties already we were short of men for the manifold requirements of a company in the line. The situation was redeemed by my splendid sergeants – and Wilson our C.S.M. A Company, alas, had lost all its officers and half its men with Peter.

Pat did the obvious thing and put Nick in to command A – my loss but of course right. Thus Nicolas achieved his captaincy, and an M.C. to boot – which will hardly surprise anyone who has read this narrative. The other two companies were fairly intact. James Dunnill was with B, but now Desmond Gethin found himself elevated to C Company. Desmond's promotion made me smile. Time cures all.

Desmond, sometimes known as "Dizzy", had been a D Company subaltern for years, and I had assumed that 17 Platoon under his presidency was a life appointment. He was a genial officer, but wore an air of vagueness which his superiors found disconcerting until they got used to it. Administration took its chance under his direction, but things usually seemed to work out somehow with the collaboration of his outstanding platoon sergeant. In Sergeant Martin, an old and valued friend of mine, and indeed of Desmond's, he lacked nothing. 17 Platoon was always a happy one, though I think they could have been half naked before Desmond noticed it. However he was certainly durable, and proved it by his battle performance on the La Bassée canal in 1940, when his platoon shot the opposition to rags with minimal fuss.

Desmond had a maddening trick of staring at the sky when receiving his orders, and one was left with vague feelings of uncertainty as to whether he had absorbed them or not. Also he was apt to conclude by saluting, with his favourite comment, "Ours not to reason why . . ." usually murmured loud enough for most of the company to hear. However they were used to it. I can understand why Lord Lucan found Cardigan difficult. Well, Desmond could now go and do the job himself. There was never anything wrong with Dizzy's performance.

Sergeant Martin had reigned in Desmond's stead, under Douglas's genial régime, since we left Scotland. A veteran of twenty-one years' service, he maintained his pre-war standards, so there were never problems with 17 Platoon while he was with us – save for that of Fusilier Given. Lance Corporal James Given, to use his part-time title, had twenty-three drunks on his fascinating series of conduct sheets. He was a regular, a leader and a true man, but his periodic promotion was only possible in contact with the enemy. Elsewhere he needed an escort – or chaining up, as Martin once sadly remarked. Of him, more later.

Then Captain Mike McDonald came as second in command. I was never so glad to have anyone. A true successor to Nick, he halved my problems immediately. Mike was commissioned from warrant rank in the Irish Guards, and he was quite outstanding. He neglected nothing, was imperturbable in action, and possessed that practical common sense which in my experience half our citizens lack entirely.

Finally we were sent an elderly subaltern, Dudley Clark. Dudley was a charming addition to the company and he entered with zest into the robust life of a platoon commander. But unfortunately he was not built for the kind of things which we were doing. It was only his bodily strength that failed him though, not his heart, and he did all that we could ever have asked of anyone, regardless of age. Moreover he earned his keep, as we sent him out into the night often enough.

Then on the 23rd we received eight reinforcements. We made a fuss of them as usual, but whether our human welcome ever compensated for our embattled surroundings I very much doubt. I know of no worse ordeal for men than to join their regiments, for the first time, in the line. They did not come with their friends as we all did, nor could they know how comradeship makes up for most circumstances, however ghastly. Of all fears, the unknown is usually the worst, but these men would be homesick and lonely too. Then their reception – mud, and a wet black night, and the vicious scream of a shell.

These were the things that rum was made for, and in later times they would think of their regiment as second only to home.

We moved back on to Grandstand again on the 22nd as a part of the general reshuffle after the London Irish battle. Gravely attenuated by the loss of a third of our strength Nelson had serious problems in holding our sector, and so we were thin on the ground. For the time being we had the whole of the hill to ourselves and could appreciate Pat's signal mark of confidence in us.

In the meantime Dudley, after a week's initiation, was now ready for battle, and we could hardly stay quiet longer after brother Koch and his tank friends' flamboyant conduct on Hill 286.

Koch shelled us rather unpleasantly on the 23rd, using mediums, their famous 5.9s, for the first time, and we lost two of our men. Some of them were getting their tea at the time and were caught above ground.

That night Dudley took a few men out on his first operation, and we sent him quite a long way across the plain to the north of Two Tree. Purely reconnaissance and partly practice, with strict orders to keep out of trouble. However Dudley was conscientious and he went well beyond his area to a small feature called Sidi Trade, a mile or two north and east of Two Tree. Here he lay up quietly with Sergeant Brandon and his men beside him, and they noticed considerable activity at the nearby farm cluster. As several vehicles came in they thought they had found a battalion H.Q., but as the Germans were then occupying most of the farms of any tactical importance across those plains it was probably no more than a platoon group or zug, which would anyway have to take in its supplies in the darkness.

Dudley came back without incident and reported, and was naturally immediately assigned the task of smashing the place up the following night. Brandon of course was overjoyed.

The operation could be described as a partial success, though like any patrol actions at night when things go wrong it was difficult to ascertain the true facts afterwards.

Dudley had taken two sections with him, about a dozen men, and they reached their target. However they were discovered by the inmates while our team was still considering the problem. The enemy shot first, and hit three of our men in the first burst. Sergeant Brandon was one of the few I ever knew capable of dealing with that kind of thing, and he shot back instantly, killing two of the opposition. The surviving members of the enemy picket promptly bolted, but as Brandon turned round with Dudley to collect his own team he found that most of them had fled also. Unabashed, Dudley proceeded in to the compound, found a truck and set it alight by the expedient of firing tracer into the petrol tank. Then after tossing a few grenades about they withdrew. A very noisy affair indeed but perhaps its message would not be lost on the opposition.

Dudley and Brandon then retreated at discretion with the two or three of their team still left to back them – rather like the ballad of the gallant Fairshon, "of whose fighting tail, just three were remainin' . . ." at his, Fairshon's, moment of truth.

However the rest of our men came in in ones or twos during the night–rather abashed, but it is no good being rough when things like that happen at night. Besides, Koch's men had fled too, and a patrol action usually ends in a sauve qui peut. Dudley had done well. And so had Sergeant Brandon, but we had lost three of our number.

Strictly speaking, Fred White was platoon sergeant of 16 Platoon under Nicolas, but latterly Nick was usually acting as second in command of the company. For most of the time, therefore, Fred was the platoon commander with Brandon as his assistant. They were a formidable pair.

Sergeant Fred White, or Chalky to the initiated, was an immaculate N.C.O. and he managed to convey an air of superiority and polished refinement under virtually all circumstances. He was probably like that by inclination, but Nick set him the example.

Brandon was very different, though both were ruthless disciplinarians. Brandon was the first choice in D Company for anything really nasty, and it was a role that he gave the appearance of actively enjoying. He combined shrewd judgment with quick reactions and his ability with weapons was quite exceptional. Brandon owed his third stripe to his personal qualities rather than to his functions.

Dudley was certainly in good hands with these two to back him, but I think he wondered what on earth he had landed up in with these two pugnacious subordinates. Moreover they were quite undisturbed by their last night's performance. Merely another thing to chalk up and another lesson learned, though there were a few ruderies flung at their luckless fusiliers who had bolted.

Before that night had ended the Germans brought some tanks up and started to shell us, but they did not press the point, knowing perhaps by then that we were mined in on Grandstand. Our own artillery replied, and when they eventually withdrew they left one of their number behind them – too far out for us to do anything about it in daylight, and the enemy recovered their winged duck the following night.

We were now perfectly aware that there was something like a cut and thrust duel going on between the Irish Brigade and Koch's battle group opposite, and the activities we were indulging in were repeated all round our front.

Douglas took one of his sections out the next night to another near-in hump, Bir Rabal, and got mixed up in an inconclusive fire fight at rather long range. However the opposition made off, and Douglas brought back one of their Schmeissers.

Later that night there was further excitement, which turned into light relief. While I was cross-examining Douglas and his warriors we were amazed to see the lights of a vehicle approaching at speed down the dark miles of the Goubellat road which stretched out across no man's land before us.

Fascinated we watched its approach, our minds working overtime as it did so. Then entering our zone it went up in a hideous series of explosions as it drove over our mines. Then a pall and a spume of smoke, followed by bits dropping, then silence. Curious, we went down to inspect, but with circumspection and sensing some new product of Koch's distorted sense of humour. We need not have worried.

We found two very dead Italians with a load of what was apparently the night's rations for the team opposite. None the less it was intriguing that they had managed to drive down the whole length of no man's land with their headlights on – across the entire divisional front in fact, without anybody minding.

Evidently these heroes had misread their maps on leaving Tunis, but if they could do that kind of thing, perhaps there were others prepared to do it less conspicuously and with more sinister intentions.

On the next night, 27 January, Brandon went out to Bir Rabal again as we thought the Germans were interested in the place after Douglas's experience the previous night. However this time it was unoccupied.

The following night was shambolic, as Douglas got mixed up in an anti-personnel minefield near Two Tree Hill, and was extremely lucky to get out of it without setting off any of these inhuman devices.

On the 29th Sergeant Brandon took his own section out to Sidi Trade again, a week having gone by since 16 Platoon's last visitation. This time he did not quite reach the area as he encountered a German picket on the way. Brandon saw them first, outlined against the sky, and feeling already committed he crawled up and tossed a grenade in. On this occasion he did not pause to investigate, as other posts opened up on them accompanied by Very lights and star shells.

After these adventures I thought that they needed a rest, and we stayed quiet for the next two nights, with 18 Platoon providing our standing posts during the night, a quarter of a mile out in that arena with the earth and rock white in the moonlight, with vision for miles except for the shadows.

At the end of the month Wilson was stricken. Our stout-hearted sergeant major had never flagged or failed, and he had bestowed his cordial abuse freely and fairly to all of our team. Older than most of us, these conditions had found out the weak spots. In pain for some time, he finally collapsed with a duodenal. Bill Edwards, our M.O., had one look, and Bert Baker the M.I. sergeant took a further one, and between them they packed him off there and then. Tug Wilson was distraught, but I am not sure which of us was the sorrier.

In this respect Sergeant Bert Baker's status requires comment. Bert was the Faugh's medical sergeant, and one of the best known N.C.Os. of the battalion. As a wit and raconteur he was in a class by himself, even among Irishmen who could appreciate such talent, and sooner or later most of them experienced it personally when destiny caught up with them and they made Bert's professional acquaintance.

I can imagine his ancestors busy with Wellington's men, slapping a pint of rum down them before setting to work with hacksaw and boiling pitch. Bert's methods were equally direct and practical. As he often said, he had quite a job working with our succession of regimental doctors who were no match for their redoubtable sergeant until they got to know his little ways. The Faugh sick rate was always low and Bert saw that it was so.

Recently I asked him for his extensive records, which had no doubt been written up carefully during the long slack periods in the R.A.P. Bert exploded. He said that he had never written up anything in the whole campaign, and the only time he ever picked up a pencil it was a blue indelible one to write "M" on the foreheads of his patients when he had slugged them with morphia, so that the professors further down the line would refrain from doing likewise.

The loss of our sergeant major was not something that could be sorted out within the company save on a temporary basis, and

Pat Scott took this opportunity to promote Fincham, James's colour sergeant in B Company. We were extraordinarily lucky and the whole company knew it, though I cannot recall poor James Dunnill's remarks about his loss. Fred Fincham was an old friend of mine and everyone liked him. Very different in disposition to Wilson, he held the reins of discipline lightly, but just as effectively.

That night, 28 January, Martin and some of 17 Platoon were out, and found the enemy laying those foul anti-personnel mines around us. Bestial things, wired together, which jumped in the air when contacted. There they exploded like shrapnel.

I never liked mining, either by our side or by the enemy, and our men detested this double-edged weapon which put defence in a straitjacket. All war is confusion and I should not be suprised if we lost more men by our own mining than by that of the enemy. I dare say that the 10th Panzer Division opposite shared my sentiments when Wolfgang Fischer their commander died that way two days later. He and his division had had a rough two years, first in Russia and then sent here – for rest and recuperation in Tunisia. A few days later Fischer was succeeded by Oberst Fritz Freiherr von Broich, who had already earned his keep by his performance at the battle of Tebourba.

That night was not one of our best ones. There will always be the odd five per cent who cannot take it, and in the whole campaign we had four of our men who deserted their colours and, perhaps worse, two S.I. wounds. We had one of these that night – a self-inflicted injury; the common method being for the misguided soldier to discharge his rifle through his foot. This character was Fusilier Mallon's number two in 16 Platoon.

Dudley and Sergeant Fred White brought Mallon over to see me. He was clearly very angry, but he saluted and reported. His speech began with the facts, but went on to cover his indifferent opinion of the man, his life history and all his works, and ended with a formal request for my permission to finish off his late comrade. He said it would be a pleasure.

I thanked Mallon for his comments, expressed my sympathy, but regretted that H.M. regulations prevented acceptance of his public-spirited offer. Of Fusilier Mallon, more later.

On 2 February we resumed our private offensive, and knowing

the Germans' obsession about the place we thought it was time that Two Tree Hill had further attention. It would also be an excellent opportunity for Corporal Robbie Robinson to justify the third stripe that he was just putting up. He was still only eighteen.

By midnight Douglas, Robbie and five others of 17 Platoon were sitting low down on the side of the feature and resting from their exertions. They had got on to the steep northern slope without any trouble, though the area was an extremely trying one due to its deep gullies and fissures. These were usually strewn with loose rock and scree which made silent movement impossible. Still, it is amazing what you can get away with at night and, if you cannot be quiet, at least be quick.

As they recovered their breath they heard voices going round them, apparently in a circle, and after poking about a bit they discovered that they were in the centre of a U-shaped wadi. Furthermore they soon realised that it was held at each end by opposition sentries whose brothers were evidently dining in front of them, in the centre of the U.

According to Robbie there was a fair amount of debate before proceeding to action. However they eventually left part of the patrol in situ to cover them while the rest crawled forward to see what they could do about the dinner party.

It was a pretty bright night and they found themselves crawling over stubble. Anyone who has done that will know that it is about as silent as a steam roller crushing fresh gravel. However they got within five or ten yards of their target when an officer climbed out of the wadi and immediately shrieked "Achtung", plus all the other compliments commonly used by the German army on those occasions. Robbie immediately fired half a magazine at the fellow, and the others followed up by lobbing grenades in. That done they packed up their traps and fled, picking up the covering party who fled with them.

There was a gratifying series of explosions to cheer their flight, then a pause, and silence, before the sky erupted in parachute flares and the usual M.G. fire flying in all directions. They paused for a while a few hundred yards back from the scene of the crime and watched the reactions. Then they set off home. The return trips were usually fast ones on these occasions.

The layman might wonder how it was that our soldiers faced so many night enterprises with equanimity, or be mystified by our ability to move freely and surely over the Tunisian wastes in the dark hours. Most of the technique was acquired by patient instruction among the Ayrshire hills, and I think that the Faughs had achieved an exceptional standard of training in night work before we ever came to this country. Thereafter practice bred confidence, but our abilities in this respect were not necessarily general throughout the army. We lost our own men often enough as has already been seen, usually in the confusion and pandemonium of night actions, but elsewhere there were cases of complete patrols wandering inadvertently into enemy positions.

Night time of course loses its terrors with familiarity, and darkness is only relative. The human system becomes used to most things under compulsion or habit, and the black night provided us with both a cloak for our designs against the enemy and the mask of invisibility to protect us from his weapons. For these simple and very obvious reasons we lived and had our being by night, and our eyes and senses adjusted themselves by all the miracles of adaptation. Living like this in the dark one could see perfectly well even on the darkest nights, and the black night is black only by contrast.

There were varying degrees of darkness in Tunisia, and to begin with, in the winter months, we were quite glad to have clouds as we crept about in the hills. The rainy spells gradually dwindled away as January progressed, and from February onwards the nights were usually bright ones under the exceptional brilliance of the stars in that climate. Once the moon was up the countryside turned to silver, and with a near desert type of reflection from the white ground one could see for miles – save down the sights of a rifle.

We preferred night operations to fighting by daylight, if for no other reason than that we felt much safer ; we knew with the mantle of darkness around us that we were never facing aimed fire unless we were stupid enough to provide a skyline target, and only when the enemy made that error was it ever possible to use the sights of our own weapons. Even then one's eyes played tricks, as the sky seemed to vanish in a shimmering opaqueness where it blended with Mother Earth, however light it might seem in the firmament above.

Under these circumstances it is not surprising that most night actions were fought out at a range of a few yards, or that our adversaries made such generous use of grenades.

The other tactical factors of night operations were of even greater importance than the blinding of the enemy's weapons. When the tide at last turned we were usually the aggressors and we held the card of surprise. We knew what we were doing and, at any given moment, more or less where we were. But the enemy could not be sure of either of these things. Moreover he probably no longer knew where his own people were once we were in, or through, his forward defences. Ignorant of the fate of his own men he was often to act on surmise or panic, and then we witnessed the fascinating spectacle of our adversaries firing in to each other or, even more important in moments of crisis, failing to fire at all.

All is confusion at night anyway, and there was little chance of the defending commander having any assessment of the tactical picture until daybreak. In consequence the adage about destiny's generosity to the bold was likely to be truer of night attacks than of any other military operations.

Our world at night was indeed another world, detached from all daytime reality. Always there was a strange sense of remoteness and spiritual isolation, like being in a dream landscape in which nothing lived save oneself and the warriors lying motionless beside one. These circumstances drew men very close together.

The whole broken terrain of Tunisia added to the general sense of illusion. On those bright nights with the moon up the deception was absolute, with the landscape apparently devoid of cover. But always there were shadows, and dips were invisible. Then movement alone was a betrayer, while a man lying still in the open, even in the light of a flare, only looked like a rock. Night indeed is a deceiver, lulling and distorting the senses until imagination takes over from reason. Never was it safe to rely solely on sentries, and in the line in the dark hours there was little rest for the officers.

We had been back on Grandstand for over a week now and I must say that we felt infinitely safer than in the earlier days, with

PLATE 5

Brigadier T. P. D. Scott, C.B.E., D.S.O. Commander of the Irish Brigade in Italy. Photograph taken in 1944.

PLATE 6

Oberstleutnant Walter Koch, Kdr. Fallschirmjäger Regiment 5 - The Fifth Parachute Regiment of the German Army. Photograph presented by one of his gefreiters while being entertained at author's company H.Q., night of 28 February 1943.

a belt of dannert wire across the whole of those forward slopes, mostly put down by the industrious Inniskillings. Also Pat had got the pioneers to cut a slit diagonally through the top of the feature, so that it was oblique to the enemy view. As the spine of the ridge was the living rock this had taken some doing, even involving our pioneers using explosives. However it was now possible to crawl over when visiting forward positions, hidden from the interested eyes opposite. These posts were eerie enough at any time, but no movement of any kind was possible in daylight. Spending hours there myself, it gave the most utter sense of isolation that I ever knew.

There were also the German dead for company. They lay everywhere on our front after the battle, and something had to be done about them.

After dark I went out with Sergeant White and a few others. There in front of the wire, among those fallen men of the Fatherland, I thought this was about as wretched a job as ever fell to the lot of a soldier. I came across a dead German officer, already on a stretcher and half bandaged, with the two stretcher bearers lying dead across him – testimony in death of their devotion. Few things have affected me more, and I returned perhaps more thoughtful than usual.

Later we did in fact bury about twenty-five of them, on two successive nights. An anxious and long drawn out business under the stars, with two covering parties nearby, and the thoughts of our men as the only honour we could pay them. On the first night there was a visitation, and out of the darkness from enemy lips came the soft call of "Faugh a Ballagh". We had been watched.

But this time no one fired.

On the second night our guardian angels saved us from tragedy, when the burial party with Mike McDonald missed its route homewards and came in from the wrong direction. Robbie was in charge of the in-lying picket covering our front while the operation was in progress. In the late night, noticing the shadows approaching, with seconds only for decisions and action, he whispered his orders. Intuition alone saved him, and before firing to kill he put a short burst of tracer above them – and Mac flung himself flat, and answered.

Night activities were often tense, and this one more than most. Robbie said later that it was the hell of a game getting the pins back into his grenades afterwards, for the night, for once, was a dark one.

Writing to father after this I said, "My dear Pop.... Am getting good at astronomy as a result of constant association with the stars for company, and I don't have to bother about looking at my watch at night now. The stars are very bright here and Orion and his dogs are a wonderful sight. Saw Scorpio the other night. We just get a glimpse of him before dawn, though very much south – that is very close to the Southern Cross. . . . One has to come to a spot like this to appreciate the things that matter in life. Funnily enough they are all simple – comfort and a home, and a life of one's own choosing, being able to sleep in a bed at nights, baths and some decent port . . . I expect that you have felt this way before now, but don't think we aren't enjoying this life – it is a great adventure, and much more comedy than tragedy ; though I doubt if the pure Nordic types over the hill feel that way. They must be kind of depressed now and they don't get much rest. . . . At the moment am in better quarters than usual. A place where an Arab kept his cow. It is greatly improved with sandbags.

". . . Nicolas is doing well with A. – a worthy successor to Peter. Strange what an effect these conditions have on folks. Most of my N.C.Os. have revealed themselves in colours one didn't suspect in peace . . . they really are darn good and greatly exceeded expectations. The warriors themselves have been magnificent. . . .

". . . Glad to hear you are providing a home for some more Canadians. I bet they are enjoying themselves."

Save for the continual thrust and counter thrust at night, the conditions of this period could have been said to be static – but I don't think that our fusiliers thought so.

7

The Second Battle of Bou Arada

THE PAUSE WHICH followed Koch's recent onslaught on us was an essential one for both sides. His Jäger veterans had suffered severely and needed time to assimilate their new boys, but the rest of the 10th Panzer Division had not been engaged to the same extent and were relatively unscathed. However the loss of their divisional commander and chief of staff on the same day, 1 February, may well have played its part in that interlude, and nearly a week elapsed before Von Broich could be made available to take over.

As for ourselves, our own losses were probably higher than the enemy's, due to the virtual destruction of one of our regiments in the Hill 286 counter attack. Far higher if one considers the long-term consequences and how these affected every one of us.

Generalleutnant Wolfgang Fischer's last battle for Germany was no mean swan song, and our London Irish Rifles were so badly smashed up in that fling as the battle ended that there was little left to count on. The losses had been ghastly, and the scene darkened by the way they had happened. There were also shock and other factors which touched on the innermost core of men's spirits – all of which could be chalked up to the enemy. This was their method in France, this the Blitzkrieg, the sure recipe for victory, and they would indeed win if men gave way to it.

For these reasons the underlying trouble involved more, and much more, than our casualties. With only a handful of their old guard left, and reinforcements thrown in as makeweight, only time could heal. Time, and effort and devotion in the end, would knit all together again to the old standards. But time above all was needed. Meanwhile stability was impossible, until the inner scars had healed, without which the confidence to fight, and endure and win battles, could never be found.

For practical purposes Nelson now had to carry on the battle with two battalions instead of three, with his rugged Inniskillings and ourselves, but the partnership was historic and known to be durable. Nothing could appal Nelson anyway. His battered riflemen now set to work to pick up the pieces and rebuild their shattered ranks, comforted I hope by the thoughts of their luckier brethren who could easily have shared their fate.

However there were larger matters afoot now, beyond Oberst Koch's ken and, I fancy, ours too. With Rommel's army driving back on its springboard in Tunisia, Von Arnim, and no doubt Hitler himself, realised that little time was left to them and strategic necessity required that they broke the First Army without further ado. This done, "the insolent Montgomery" could have their undivided attention. The latter was now rapidly approaching the southern frontier and in a few more days would be battering on the gates of Mareth.

Mind you, we were not very happy about Monty's activities. The more he pushed, the greater was the compression, and all we found was that we had ever increasing hordes of Rommel's warriors on our front. Moreover we were the weak point and they knew it.

These were the thoughts, and the circumstances, which led to the next adventures, and our brigade had the honour of holding the centre when Von Arnim's new offensive broke upon us. The bard I think got his words twisted when extolling King Louis' men, and writing that "the right of the van is the Irish Brigade". Still, we all knew what he meant. It usually was, and it was so now.

At the beginning of February Nelson had had one of his periodic bouts of intuition and, as he mentioned later in his own writings, he sensed the evil intentions of our adversaries. I think that he had nothing to go on other than his own appreciation based on his inner feelings, and I very much doubt if he had any really positive intelligence information from higher sources. Had there been any such, it was never apparent and it never reached us on the ground in the forward positions. The strategic surprise when it came was a total one, and Von Arnim certainly achieved that even if he bungled everything else.

During this period Nelson became obsessed with the desire for a reserve. This was unknown hitherto as the entire army's goods were permanently in the shop window. We did not even have a spare company. Writing of it later Nelson said that he was considerably criticized for his outmodish, erratic and unusual attitude to war in North Africa. Admittedly it was difficult to create a reserve in view of what had lately happened to his brigade, but none the less he did so, and he pulled out half of the Faughs for his purpose. D Company were one half of the half, and A Company the other. A and D Company habitually worked together.

Nelson as usual was quite right. The enemy were thickening up on our front. Evidence of this from patrol reports was continual and cumulative, night by night, showing that most of the farms in the plains around us were becoming occupied. We were soon to learn that they were behind us too. The hostile tide was flowing wherever we could not contain it.

With these thoughts Nelson thinned out his front on the night of 22 February, and pulled A Company and ourselves back to Djelida, leaving Pat with half the battalion forward.

I had sent Mike McDonald on earlier with the colour sergeant, Dave Bartlett, and his minions, to study our new location and to have our reception, evening meal and all else, ready for the company on its arrival that night. The place was several miles back behind us, or rather westwards of our positions. There was no rear in our war in Tunisia.

I never liked night withdrawals from the line. They were always tense and dangerous during the hand-over phase, and that night was blacker than usual. As we withdrew at nightfall the enemy started to shell us with their mediums, and hurrying somewhat I nearly took the company through one of our own minefields in the darkness. It was a cross-country trek, all the way by compass, as it would have been far too hazardous to plod down the main road past the end of the sinister Hill 286. All was uncertain anyway, as all land was no man's land that one did not happen to occupy.

Our new position lay close to the Bou Arada-El Aroussa road, which ran east-west about a half mile below us. This road could be described as the right flank or frontier of the Irish Brigade positions, but it lay immediately below the southern ramparts of the colossal mountain mass of Djebel Rihane, which soared up above us like a scrub-laden and dirty edition of Ben Lomond.

I did not like it very much, being overhung like that.

I posted the company in a kind of square formation in a fairly solid block of cactus, and Mac and I spent an hour or two with the fusiliers, pulling dannert wire round the site. Then we set the 2″ mortars at high angle near the corners, with their parachute flares beside them and a pair of Brens as well. After that we felt somewhat safer. I don't think Nick put up wire, and I ought to have warned him – with intuition ringing all its alarm bells inside me.

The next morning I sent Douglas Walsh up in to the hills at our back with part of 17 Platoon, to have a look round, but this was by way of our own security and they did not go high up to search out the summits. However they found no signs of human activity and were back in the late afternoon, hot and frustrated, and thinking the whole operation pointless.

Later that night there was anxious enquiry from brigade headquarters, who evidently knew or suspected some devilment; meantime please continue our searching.

That night I went to sleep in pyjamas for the first time, and the last, in this campaign – but it was not a restful night. In the morning I sent Sergeant Fred White further into the Djebel with Brandon's section, and a few others of 16 Platoon. In an hour or two came the distant sounds of small arms reverberating down the slopes, and echoing back like the shots from the top guns on our Perthshire hills in August.

They came in later. My cousin James Browne had come to dine with us. James was second in command of one of 132 Field Regiment's batteries and we thought at least we ought to entertain our gunners on suitable occasions. James was entertained further as Brandon staggered in with two worried looking Jäger prisoners, and carrying a third, alas, mortally wounded, all from 1st J.R.H.G.

It was quite a tale, as Fred and Brandon had actually passed these people lying up unseen, but they had a rear file of a pair of fusiliers a hundred yards behind the rest of the patrol. The Germans came out from cover in time to collide with our toiling rearguard. Exchanging affectionate sentiments and explaining that they were Americans the Germans turned aside and our warriors continued on – and then the penny dropped. They whipped round and both parties reached for their guns. Brandon whipped round too, and in a trice had discharged an entire Bren magazine into them. The Germans flung themselves flat, then rose to their feet with their hands up – save for the one who could not, and a couple of others who fled.

This dying German soldier – he was only about twenty – said to me in James's presence what a pity they had to fight us, for we were such gentlemen —

This was not the end of the matter and we should have known it. The worst things happened when the moon was bright, but now a distant storm which had been muttering and grumbling around us during the evening burst into a full scale thunderstorm over us. Around midnight the Arab dogs were barking all down and around the mountain side; and then nearby, first hysterically and then after a while in ones and twos, dying fitfully away into uneasy silence.

A short lull followed, but our posts were manned and our men alert. Suddenly a series of orange flashes lit up A Company's area below us. Then a burst of Schmeisser fire followed. Then more bursts, until they all ran in together, mixed with an endless succession of grenade explosions and Very lights.

We put up our parachute flares but there was not even a sign of movement between us and A Company, nor anything to see anywhere in the dark mass of the olive trees and the murk of the storm. Nor could we have fired at that stage without hitting A Company.

Of course they had come in from the other side, a dozen or so German paratroopers simply charging through A Company and firing as they went. Most of the company were asleep after their recent exertions. They killed Nick's batman, and quite a number of others, and went on their way unscathed after inflicting seventeen casualties. It was a very bold action, typical of the troops we were fighting and Koch's way of thinking, and it was another classic instance of the effective use of surprise.

Nick came over later, much upset and blaming himself. But it is no good doing that in war – only to learn the lesson, and we had to expect these things from our brave and resolute enemy.

This however was art and part of the larger proceedings, and at first light we knew that Von Arnim was attacking our army from Bou Arada to the sea.

We of course, with A Company, were immediately called forward, and joined up with battalion headquarters below Djebel Rihane on its eastern slopes – very convenient at this central point of the Irish Brigade perimeter. We could counter attack, with equal rapidity, penetration by the enemy from any direction – Stuka Ridge, Grandstand or southwards to Bou Arada. Nelson's policy was paying off, but unfortunately he was no longer there to appreciate it. Pat reigned in his stead.

There had also been some changes in enemy dispositions. Von Broich had gone on south with most of the 10th Panzer Division and was now busy assisting Rommel against the Americans at Sbeitla. However the same old team was still opposite us at Bou Arada, save that there were now more of them and they were under the command of Oberst Joseph Schmid, whose Hermann Göring Division was now pretty well complete, and included part of the 7th Panzers who had caused all the trouble on Hill 286.

Koch was naturally still with us, with an independent battle group composed of his own regiment of paratroopers and a battalion of the J.R.H.G., and apparently answerable only to Von Arnim himself; that is if the generaloberst could be said to be in control of events just then.

Strictly speaking this was Rommel's battle, for the generalfeldmarschall had taken command of both armies at its outset, and only handed over when he had irrevocably lost it. Then, significantly, Rommel went on sick leave, while his luckless subordinate reaped the consequences. But Jürgen von Arnim's enforced spell afterwards as a British guest was a happier ending than being poisoned by the Führer, and Rommel's fate at the hands of Hitler is one of the foulest blots in the infamous history of the Third Reich. Erwin

Rommel's murder illustrates perfectly how evil men with absolute power will not endure genius or valour, in those who serve them, but only crawlers and sycophants.

While we were making our own moves, away to the south of us at Sbeitla and Kasserine, Rommel's men had broken through and had virtually obliterated the American forces pushing at his sensitive western flank. Rommel's purpose of course was to ensure that they played no further part in proceedings while he made good his junction with the 5th Panzer Army up north. Meanwhile Von Arnim could get on with the job of liquidating the British after the excellent start he had given them. We were now to witness a much larger and more thorough attempt to roll up our line from the bottom.

The German offensive on our front began with their usual enterprise on 26 February. During the preceding nights Schmid and his minions had taken a substantial armoured force over the Goubellat plain and across the mountain barrier, and as dawn broke on the 26th our rear headquarters at El Aroussa found themselves very much in the firing line. Nelson was hauled back to cope, and scratch forces of every class, kind and colour, were rushed to him to hold the passes. While these disturbances were going on behind us, the Irish Brigade was left in Pat Scott's capable hands, and the Faughs with Beauchamp.

On our front the London Irish were holding our old positions on the northern escarpment – along Stuka Ridge and the adjoining features. Here on those steep and well-protected ridges it was thought they were reasonably secure after their recent disaster. Still in embryo, and with young riflemen who scarcely yet even knew each other, new ordeals were unthinkable, defensive or otherwise.

Oberst Koch made a bee line for them.

Here at first light on 26 February 1943 our London Irish Rifles in skeleton strength, and the rest of the brigade, were set upon by the second battalion of the Jäger Regiment Hermann Göring, and by most of Koch's 5th Parachute Regiment in combination with them. There were also several other infantry units of uncertain ancestry attached to the paras, about six battalions in all.

The northern sector immediately collapsed under the onslaught. The Rifles fought it out manfully, but were speedily engulfed. However, to their lasting credit, two of their companies held firm, and this key area became the scene of an infantry conflict where, by nightfall, both sides had lost control of their troops and their grip on events.

With the enemy in and through the London Irish positions, and most of that vital ridge in their possession, our gunners below and beyond them were firing into their opponents in a ninety degree arc over open sights, a practice which all good gunners consider unprofessional, or even barbarous, if at times necessary. It was certainly necessary now, as they sweated behind their weapons under the direct fire of Koch's Spandaus.

The fighting went on all through the night, and at first light Beauchamp counter attacked our broken front. James Dunnill, with B Company, went in on Stuka Ridge with several tanks of the North Irish Horse, with Nicolas and A Company over on his left. Nick diverged away, up and on to the higher slopes to the north-west. Both counter attacks succeeded. Nick had no trouble, as the enemy bolted as soon as our artillery opened on them and they saw what was afoot. These were the lesser fry, Koch's second string, but B Company's antagonists fought it out. They were the J.R.H.G. and true to form, but they could not cope with our tanks.

After a sharp fire fight the Jägers decided in favour of discretion and made off, but not far and just outside the vision of the North Irish Horse tanks perched on the top of the escarpment. Mixed up with the surviving posts of the London Irish, they had little chance of holding, and the course of the battle on our front shows how a few groups that stick it out can paralyse a large-scale offensive.

That night Desmond Gethin had the wretched task of taking some of C Company out to clear the battlefield, and to pick up the injured soldiers of both sides who were scattered over the grim slopes of Stuka Ridge. This was always a tense business, and usually safer in daylight when the enemy could see what was happening, and forbear accordingly, and when we could see for ourselves.

Desmond had a covering force out with his subaltern Jimmy

Clarke, later famous in Faugh annals, but this night, grisly enough anyway in view of what they were doing, Desmond and Jimmy came very near to killing our doctor, Bill Edwards, who was out with his minions on mercy bent but without apparently telling anyone first.

The following day there was help from another source – a German paratrooper Hans Teske joining in and recovering one of our men and several of his own through one of our minefields. A gallant feat which unfortunately earned him a machine gun bullet from our side and, most justly, the Iron Cross from his own.

While these chastening events were in progress, and our own front line stabilising again, Beauchamp moved us up in the bed behind B Company. Then the next morning Dick Jefferies came over for breakfast. Dick, Nicolas' brother, was adjutant now, as Nelson had borrowed Charles O'Farrell as staff captain in the aftermath of our previous battle. Dick mentioned later that his unexpected honour was conferred at an hour's notice on Grandstand when he was second in command of A Company, otherwise destiny would have taken him with Peter that evening of 18 January against the J.R.H.G. But all soldiers can think of the "ifs", and who can say what Dick's quiet restraint could have done that day.

Dick brought the news that we were required to divert the enemy that night and that the C.O. wanted to talk about it. So I went back with him, to find a relaxed Beauchamp, and asked for my instructions. My revered commanding officer blinked at me, and to the best of my recollection said, "You can do what you like, my dear chap, only get out on that plain and create as much trouble as you can think up." This of course was striking across enemy communications, and Beauchamp pointed out that the Germans were still in action ten miles behind us, so there was pretty wide scope. There was not in fact a great deal to discuss, with the situation perfectly plain to both of us – and the purpose obvious.

I saluted and went back to the company, not particularly bothered. With a wide discretion like that, and given only the intention, it would be my own fault if anything went wrong. The dangerous part was at the beginning where B Company, guarding as it were the passes, were in fairly close contact with the enemy.

We should have to go through them, knowing that the J.R.H.G. scouts were watching them closely – perhaps only a pistol shot from them once the darkness descended.

I got hold of Brandon, told him he had a night's work ahead of him, and asked him to collect up a dozen men each from 16 and 17 Platoon – that is about four reduced sections. When he had rounded the team up I explained what was expected of us and gave them a few details about our mode of progression, and the usual tactical points common on these occasions. Then as the light faded we set out, carrying a pair of Brens with us in addition to our usual armament.

We cleared B Company, having arranged with James a few recognition details for our return, and then ploughed on northwards in to the starry night – in hops, with a rear party covering us. To begin with we made enough noise ourselves to awaken the dead as we climbed down over the scree, and we were not sorry for what was going on in the background.

Dusk is a risky period for starting missions, as both sides suspect devilment then and are liable to assert themselves. In consequence there was plenty of activity when we said goodbye to James. Sporadic shelling was falling on Grandstand and on our other positions in the vicinity; however once off Stuka Ridge and plunging down the escarpment we soon left the noises of battle behind us. Distant gunfire somehow enhances feelings of remoteness, and especially so when moving with set and sinister purpose in no man's land. Then there are no sounds save of one's own making, or imagining, and the whine of distant shells and their dull impersonal explosions blend with one's tensions to create some kind of mental harmony. I know that stress is at its highest when all is quiet – though that did not happen often over our front at Bou Arada.

We had travelled perhaps a mile before making the first and often fatal mistake of accidental collision with the enemy at night. The silence was absolute and I had heard nothing, but coming over a small rise from almost under my nose came that searing German challenge – almost a shriek, with fear wrapped in it. I dropped flat, but not so Brandon beside me. With his instant reactions his grenades went flying long before he dived for cover. Too late by a whisker, those interminable seconds followed, and the German picket fired the longest burst that I ever heard. Then came the explosions, two of them, followed by momentary silence, broken this time by the cries of badly injured men, in front as well as beside us.

I inched back on my toes. Brandon was hit, and several others. Bartram crept up behind me and whispered, "We can get them, sir, if we go in now." But I said not, thinking of others behind them, perhaps ready and waiting. We pulled back our four injured men, by their ankles I think, and drew back and round westwards to a nearby fold. Here we dealt with our casualties, quietened with morphia where needed, but Brandon, hit in the shoulder, mercifully could walk, and Brandon would get them home. I sent half the team back with him.

With Bartram and Robbie beside me now and both our Brens, we went on northwards until we came to a well-used cross track. Thinking it promising, we lay up to wait on events, one of those French farm steadings near and below us, silent and sinister under the star canopy above it. Not even a distant gun was firing now.

Perhaps an hour passed by, or less, for time is deceiving, then down from the hills from the west came one of the German heavy lorries, which were twice the size of our own machines. We heard the low rumbling of its approach long before it came in view, and even then saw the dust clouds before the machine emerged from them, coming at us like a charging mastodon. At the range of a few feet we fired the complete magazines from the two Brens into it, and our whole team followed suit with their rifles. I discharged my tommy gun into the cab, but after a few rounds the damnable thing jammed.

As to the lorry, the results were impressive; travelling fast in the bright night it went hard over and into the wall of the farm, like the sound of a shell burst. There was the brief scream of tortured metal and the sound of falling bricks, then silence – utter and complete, but not for long.

We reloaded and, noticing the background noises below us, withdrew discreetly a short distance up the track. There we settled down again and waited, conscious for the first time that the night was a cold one.

Later – very much later and seemingly after an hour or more, we heard further slight sounds about us and nearby, but for an interminable pause nothing followed them. Then it happened all too quickly as several shadows emerged out of the gloom ahead, coming straight towards us swiftly and silently. My hand on the corporal's shoulder, our men lay motionless, Mallon with the Bren in his shoulder beside me. At perhaps twenty yards Mallon fired and, excitement for once overcoming him, put his burst straight over the top of the enemy. Perhaps it was just as well, for the Germans flung themselves flat as the rest of our men let rip. Every one of us missed, save for a single unlucky shot, and after this regrettable display of incompetence and indiscipline Corporal Bartram stood up, walked a few yards forward, and quietly called to the enemy. Getting to their feet they came over to us, save for their comrade who lay there dead.

In spite of their experience the Germans were calm enough, and both saluted politely. Both could speak perfect English and both were Jäger gefreiters. Bartram with perfect courtesy even went through the motions of introducing them. I said to them, "Will you swear on your honour as German soldiers that you will not attempt to escape?" They swore this appeal without hesitation, and then joining the patrol walked back beside me. However, one of them mentioned to Robbie, by way of conversation, that he didn't think we were very good shots.

Nothing could now be done as there was not a lot of night left to us. Moreover our opponents around us could safely be assumed to be wakeful. So, looking up and seeing friendly Orion above the distant hills, I knew he would steer us home.

Nearing B Company our men burst into song – "Slattery's Mounted Foot" or some other damn foolery. So at least James knew who was coming. One of the gefreiters observed that our people seemed to be a cheerful lot.

And so, home.

The remainder of the night we spent with Mac, David Bartlett and several of the others, entertaining our guests. They had rather a lot of rum. One of them said how much they liked being on the British front. He had just returned from Russia, and he gave me a photograph of his chief. Both of them clearly adored Koch. They also mentioned that there had been eighteen men in that lorry. By the dawn I think they would have changed sides for tuppence. However Beauchamp said that divisional intelligence were vexed as they could get nothing out of the men. I am not surprised. They were exceedingly drunk when they left us, and were probably suffering from hangovers.

During the morning Dick Jefferies asked me over to lunch. He said, "The C.O. wants you to do it again tonight, but it is information this time and Beauchamp says you've got to be quiet after making all that noise last night."

I told Corporal Bartram that I should want him again with a section of 18 Platoon, and then went over to the battalion headquarters. Beauchamp was away with Pat, who was still acting brigadier, so I spent an hour talking to Dick. He said, "Bad luck, old boy, but really they were quite pleased about last night and naturally expect you to repeat the performance."

Then Beauchamp appeared. He explained that they wanted to find out what was going on behind the battle which was still raging, away on our northern flank, and whether or not the Germans were reinforcing that twelve-mile-long thrust they had made through the First Army front.

Nelson was still resisting this intrusion behind us with a strange international army which included French colonial troops, an American combat team, and some Churchill tanks. There was also an unlikely leavening of the mixture when the Guards Brigade were temporarily lent to him. Between them all they brought the German thrust gradually but decisively to a stop.

In a natural comment on those dearest to him Nelson remarked afterwards that they got a good deal of loot out of the battle, "and would have got a great deal more if the 3rd Grenadiers had not been part of the Brigade". A rapacious lot, he said, but the gallant guardsmen were clearly men after Nelson's own heart.

However, the battle was still apparently continuing at the full thrust of its high tide, though we did not then know that the ebb was about to set in. Beauchamp explained that Nelson was extremely interested in the enemy supply routes over those hills, presumably with a view to interception, and also to know who and what else were on their way to plague him.

Realising that there had been no pause since the last night's activities, Beauchamp perhaps blinked rather more than usual when coming to the operative part of his orders. He said that he would like me to find out what I could. Would be most grateful in fact . . . would I mind . . . and much else.

Dick had lately acquired a German-speaking Frenchman of doubtful extraction. For some unknown reason he offered me this sinister-looking character, who clearly had not shaved for weeks, and suggested that the man might be useful in the coming night's operations. I looked at the scoundrel and was inclined to agree – he might. There were perhaps possibilities so I took him back with me, and we set off immediately.

It was now about 4 p.m., and collecting Bartram and his section I gave them a brief run over my orders and the purpose of our mission. That took about five minutes and then we were off in daylight, the Frenchman with us. If the Germans had caught him they would have shot him instantly simply on the grounds of his appearance. After my own experiences last night I went in for lighter attire, as did the rest of our men, knowing that we had an arduous night ahead of us. Clad in polo-necked sweater and slacks I discarded that wretched tommy gun in favour of a pistol and a pair of grenades, but we took a Bren gun with us.

Corporal Bartram stepped naturally into Brandon's shoes, having the same aptitudes and inclination, and he assumed the role with hardly a comment on my part. There would be no repetition of high shooting tonight, not by Bartram anyway, though I had to tell him that we had got to avoid that kind of adventure altogether on this occasion if at all possible.

We went through James Dunnill's men again, spread ourselves wide in the daylight, and went fast northwards along the edge of the foothills keeping well away from the farms. As the light faded we split into two groups, with one party covering the other forward. By midnight we were ten miles out in German territory and close to Goubellat. We had not seen a soul, but Arab dogs had barked almost without cessation.

In all of this distance we had found only a single track that was beyond doubt in main use, and not even that one by tracked vehicles.

PLATE 7

Captain D. N. Jefferies, M.C.,
The Royal Irish Fusiliers.
"Nicolas".

PLATE 8

Photograph taken in May 1943, Tunisia.

Lt. Col. B. H. Butler, D.S.O., The Royal Inniskilling Fusiliers.

"Beauchamp", 2 i.c., and later C.O. of 1st Bn. Royal Irish Fusiliers in Tunisia.

Lt. Col. T. P. D. Scott, D.S.O. The Royal Irish Fusiliers.

"Pat", C.O. of 1st Bn. Royal Irish Fusiliers, and, later, of 2nd London Irish Rifles.

Brigadier N. Russell, D.S.O., M.C. The Royal Irish Fusiliers.

"Nelson", Commander of the Irish Brigade in Tunisia.

I now knew that the main effort was further north, and beyond our sector.

Watching Goubellat, we lay for a while in the foothills, listening under the light of the stars – and in fact resting as well as listening. But the whole country around us was silent as the grave, save for flickers of light in the north-east – our airmen at work no doubt. Some of our unimaginative warriors even slept, and when one came to think of it there was no reason why they should not. Most of them had not done so these last forty-eight hours, and they were probably safer ten miles behind the enemy's lines than they were in front of him.

Eventually we headed south once more, searching the farms as we reached them, with Orion our constant guide beckoning us home.

In the very late night Bartram, who was a little ahead of us, dropped suddenly. Flattened to the earth he lay motionless, save for a hand half-raised behind him in warning. Crawling up beside him I noticed the slight sounds around us and signed our men in beside me. Across our front and starkly outlined in the southern sky a German company seventy strong was marching. Perfectly drilled as usual, and all eyes glued on the next ahead, not one of them looked about him. With rifles shouldered, and wearing packs, they moved in file and perfectly spaced – a sight that would live in one's mind for ever. Those black silhouettes were rapidly marching eastwards and passing at barely a pistol shot. I counted them as they went, the Bren gun ready beside me.

Afterwards I wondered how often we had been watched like that by other curious eyes. But some of our soldiers were canny, with celtic gifts of perception, and I think that we might have known. But had those men been just a few minutes later they would have given an end-on target, and that was not to be missed whatever the need for silence.

We paused for a while and listened as they receded into the night. Below and east, and not far away, that track led by one of those farms, so we followed in the wake of the enemy and up to the edge of its compound. Feeling rather a cad I sent our French renegade in with instructions to make noises in German and attract the inmates' attention – with interesting possibilities of targets if they set on the man or chased him. I think I said we might have to shoot him if there was lack of co-operation.

The Frenchman complied as requested, and in fact made a great deal of noise ; but only silence followed – a nasty silence too. However, morally committed we had to get in there, and recovering our ill-used scallywag we rushed the place. Mindless of noise now, the place echoed back at us. Searching we found nothing save the remains of a long occupation and a large supply of hand grenades. But when we had finished the dawn had come.

The walk back over the open plain under the watchful eyes of the enemy was a tense one. In fact we raced back and arrived for breakfast, to find Beauchamp waiting in my H.Q. with Mac. Both seemed pleased to see us, thinking us a little late. It was unusual for patrols to come in several hours after first light, and I sensed apprehension, though Beauchamp was the last ever to show it.

We had been twenty miles and had upset no one and nothing, except possibly the wretched Frenchman's feelings.

We had also apparently found out what Pat and Beauchamp wanted, but that enemy company surely told us that someone was pulling out. And so in fact they were. They had had enough of Nelson.

As for the enemy, their corps commander opposite, Oberst Friedrich Weber, reporting on his own 334 Division as well as Oberst Schmid's, saw fit to mention that at the end of the battle on 1 March they had only six tanks left in service between them. They had begun it with seventy-seven.

Nelson's gunners and the Derby Yeomanry, between them, could account for some of that deficiency, but never was there more prodigal or useless waste, or such gross mishandling by our adversaries. They had used up their fighting strength and achieved nothing by it – save to hasten the ruin of their army.

8

Transition

THE STRATEGIC CONSEQUENCES of this second defensive victory in our sector were far reaching, if only that this was a battle that the Germans had to win. Von Arnim knew, and none better, that Hitler's plans had collapsed, and both he and Rommel would have done better now to have saved their armies, or a substantial part of them, while time still remained for this to be possible.

Our battle was of course but a part of a much larger operation on Von Arnim's part, and it progressively embraced the entire front of the First Army. Indeed it had begun in concert with Rommel when the adventurous field marshal set upon the Americans at Kasserine. None the less our positions in the Bou Arada sector were vital ones, and had become the southern corner-stone of the defence system. Had these fallen it is hard to know where matters might have ended with the whole of the front turned.

Until this, the second Battle of Bou Arada, the enemy had a good chance of winning. With Von Arnim's 5th Panzer Army still largely intact, and Rommel's famous desert army group concentrated together under the field marshal himself, the German forces were formidable enough and they had ample ground for thinking they could wipe the floor with us.

Half the forces opposed to them then were inexperienced or green, and the odds in German favour were far greater than they ever were in the desert battles. Why then did things go wrong? They had interior lines, advantage in numbers and a homogeneous force, which gave them the edge in quality in view of the strange assortment of the allied army. With air superiority absolute, the Germans held most of the cards, but the Gods decided against them.

Also Von Arnim's handling of affairs was less than convincing, for although Rommel was supreme commander during this phase, the generaloberst conducted the northern battle with results that were in marked contrast to Rommel's shattering blows on the southern front.

Up to this time we scarcely ever saw a British aircraft, but the Germans ranged free and unmolested.

I wondered about Michael. My brother was somewhere behind us and flying a Hurricane fighter-bomber. Mike's career was unusual as he was a Faugh himself and had been one of Quentin Findlater's subalterns in B Company in 1940. But after the French campaign he found life dull and transferred to the Air Force in search of excitement. This he had no difficulty in finding. There was a certain amount of repartee in the mess at the time on the theme of wasting valuable infantry officers in such a manner, but no doubt Winston had his reasons for allowing these postings.

A few days later a whole squadron of them came over us low, hell bent on trouble. The Stukas had temporarily vanished, but the Hurricanes were behaving viciously over the distant hills, and the noise of their cannon and other explosions was encouraging. But tracer was arcing in all directions across the sky too.

Our men read the omens. Something new was afoot.

The German sword being broken and ours yet hardly sharpened, the sector quietened. It became suspiciously quiet as the first weeks of March passed by and we could all reflect on what lay ahead. We were aware of the change of emphasis, and we all knew that the enemy power was ebbing. We also knew that our adversaries could be extremely nasty once their backs were truly against the wall. Meanwhile there was discipline and a variety of other matters to attend to if we were to be ready for the next act in the drama.

On 3 March Beauchamp moved D Company back to its counter attack role in the folds of the ridges behind Grandstand. It was quite a pleasant spot, and we took over the position from B Company in very different circumstances to that of our last handover. This time we indulged in a small cocktail party with James and his chaps, and Bob Hare the North Irish Horse troop commander, who was part of the establishment. It was quite a good place for a party, and exceedingly honorific.

We found ourselves with an ancient Roman forum as the centrepiece of the company area. The ruin itself was impressive, with the columns largely intact like a miniature Parthenon. Although severely damaged, the stonework could have been cut and erected yesterday, like the famous legend which crowned it: "Senatus Populusque Romanus", and here I held my court.

One of our fusiliers had run for it, but the would-be deserter had been caught by our own people and ignominiously brought back to us. This of course was a futile waste of time, for what use could such men ever be to us, and whoever could make cowards fight? Later the miscreant was marched in front of me by Sergeant Major Fincham. "Prisoner and escort, shun. Quick march. Halt. Left turn." Sergeant Martin slammed his rifle butt down on the man's foot as Fincham reported and called the snivelling wretch into silence, all in one sentence.

Martin and the provost corporal delivered their damning evidence to the sky over my head through the absent roof, no doubt as their counterparts had done before the Roman centurions in bygone ages.

The man had nothing to say of course. Deserters never had. I gave the man fourteen days field punishment or some other entirely illegal sentence, told Martin to make his life hell, and concluded by saying, "And now get out, you worthless rat."

The C.S.M. bellowed "Sir", and Martin repeated the tribute as his sergeant major called the man up with a command like a burst from a schmeisser. The exit was as dramatic as the entry, and the feet retreated down the length of the forum at an ever accelerating pace as Fincham's words hissed after the man, and were improved upon by Martin. They lost nothing by their echo, and I hoped the centurions were applauding from the shadows.

Shortly afterwards the C.S.M. looked in again, grinning, and said the fusilier wanted to complain to the C.O. about his treatment and the remarks I had made.

Beauchamp came round the next night, the dignity of battalion orders then being impossible. The last thing that he wanted was to be bothered by disciplinary problems in the companies, and it was up to us, his company commanders, to protect him from them.

The same formalities followed, except for the rifle butt, this time with Beauchamp presiding, while I stood beside him. He heard out the man's complaint, then asked for my comments. I gave them.

He then turned to the fusilier and, blinking, remarked, "The major has – er – called you a rat . . . and as you have behaved like one you cannot complain because he has called you one . . . I think you are – er – a rat, and I confirm the sentence."

Beauchamp then came back for a drink with us. He had just given D Company a new subaltern, Lieutenant Peter Sillem.

Peter was a swashbuckler. He had a heart of gold and he dressed like a pirate. He was a delight to serve with, and he made his mark in our little history.

I gave Peter 18 Platoon with Sergeant Murphy to hold his hand, not that Peter ever needed much guidance with men.

However, the Lord giveth and the Lord taketh away. By some unbelievably stupid edict at the highest level an army order reached us withdrawing anyone over forty from the line of battle. By this unexampled act of madness we were deprived of two of our bed-rock, Douglas Walsh and our ever faithful Sergeant Martin. Neither of these two cared particularly whether they lived or died, providing they stayed in the regiment. Mind you, I am not at all sure that "Crimes" Martin was not over fifty, let alone forty. Not that it mattered. The great Duke himself was fifty-four when he won Blenheim.

At the same time dear old Dudley took his leave. Bill Edwards took one look at him after his last patrol and sent him off for down-grading. That was a different matter, but we still missed him.

On 4 March I was president of a court martial, held in state at brigade headquarters. There were seven cases, nearly all deserters, and each took less than half an hour. Our men did not like deserters. It is not hard to understand why, and their crime with its overtone of cowardice was bitterly resented. There was the feeling of being let down and that they were deserting them, their friends and comrades – like the case of one of our mortar crews where the number one found himself without his mate or his ammunition. He said sadly that he had been personally deserted.

Occasionally there were cases which had our sympathy, where a fusilier simply aberrated after previous stouthearted service, perhaps due to a bad letter from home or temporary loss of nerve, or even through fatigue. But these cases rarely reached courts martial, not in good regiments anyway, where everyone knew each other. Usually a temporary change of scene would put matters right, such as a week or two with the mule columns. Afterwards they would be only too delighted to be safely back with their friends in the line.

Our men of course committed just as many crimes as those of other regiments, but the criminal records of the Faughs were so colourful and varied that whole sections of the Manual of Military Law required no further examples for its texts. However, disgraceful conduct was uncommon, and I could not swallow those cases in front of me that day. I gave the wretches several years penal servitude apiece and returned to D Company glad to breathe cleaner air.

The next day was Barrosa Day. The fifth of March is sacred to the Faughs, and usually a whole day is given over to celebrating this obscure encounter with Soult's men in the Peninsula. It is venerated principally as a military shambles where, in the Faugh view, they redeemed a battle which would otherwise have been lost through the ineptitude of the commander and the misconduct of the rest of the allied army. This of course is a traditional Faugh theme.

The Inniskillings have a similar peculiarity, and I notice that they are much more interested in their single-handed fight in the Caribbean – St. Lucia – than in their immortal performance at Waterloo.

I was summoned to the battalion H.Q. mess for dinner that evening, and to drink that infernal Barrosa cup, this time filled up with rum and diluted by an evil selection of liqueurs which Dick Jefferies had found somewhere. With our pipers playing around us we drank it out of a shell case, cut down and polished by our pioneers for the occasion. Nelson came over to join us.

By the middle of March we had gradually realised that our

defensive war was ending, and Nelson told us that our job in the immediate future was to break the enemy, and that he strongly suspected that our high command were going to follow the historic practice of King Louis and apply the Irish Brigade against the nastiest part of the enemy line. Nelson's intuition was again correct.

After the second Battle of Bou Arada we were transferred to the 78th Division, and we belonged to this matchless formation for the rest of the war. In later times we would be informed of a strange, if unsought, honour by enemy testimony – "that they identified the decisive sector by our presence."

Nelson now had to take some difficult personal decisions. His anxieties over the London Irish were finally determined by the grim events on 26 February. After this second catastrophic encounter with Koch's Jägers there was little choice left other than to gather up the remains.

Our riflemen might have had a chance to rebuild their broken teams had a protracted quiet defensive role been possible, unnoticed by the enemy. But there was no prospect of this as the campaign in Tunisia moved to its climax, and the future tasks of the Irish Brigade involved assaulting a formidable adversary in carefully prepared positions.

Only experience, expertise, and moral resolution could help us now, and none of this was available at short notice.

On 15 March Nelson withdrew the ailing remnants of our long-suffering riflemen, out of the line into quieter surroundings. There they would repair their damage and renew their fighting capacity. He also posted Pat Scott in to command them, and James Dunnill to help him. Naturally their feelings were not considered, but both were impervious to the caprice of fortune, and Pat's caustic wit would come to his rescue.

In the Faughs we were of course expected simply to ignore the fact of losing our best officers.

But Nelson was right as usual, and we could afford to do this having Beauchamp who had been in the saddle for a month already, and who had only to lift his little finger to be served.

15 March – "remember March, the ides of March remember",

– almost St. Patrick's Day and near enough no matter. It was not a coincidence, but it was just as well that we were leaving the sector.

Sparkling days were coming with the earliest hints of spring, and the wild geese indeed were flighting. They came off the salt lakes by Zaghouan and they flew over us, night after night, usually in the last of the light, when the setting sun was spreading its orange glow over the western sky.

They came in squadrons and they came in hundreds, in serried ranks with their flankers wavering, their endless yattering gossip disturbing the silent battlefield beneath them.

Straight over Two Tree Hill they came – and then they came over us.

One of our sentries could bear it no longer. Opening up with his Bren, our tracer went streaking ahead of the astonished birds in a golden stream of ascending droplets. A brief pause followed as our warriors appreciated the significance of the outrage, then the whole of the battalion's pickets joined in with a majestic firework display which was a perfect embroidery of the last rays of the sunset.

The birds were not bothered, and after redressing their disordered ranks they went on their way, making more noise than ever.

As for our stolid competitors on the other side of the hill, I should like to have seen the night's battle report, and heard Koch snorting into his kümmel as he discussed it.

Beauchamp said nothing. He knew it was useless.

When the First Division was arriving a few days later we had to see in the new boys. The K.S.L.I. took over our sector on Grandstand, and one of our fusiliers had the neck to remark, "A windy lot – listen to all that sporadic firing – it never happened with us."

None the less that flight of the wild geese was the direst omen for Oberstleutnant Walter Koch, and with their passage westwards his distinguished career ended in the murky twilight that shrouded so many of the star characters of the German army.

On 18 March he was recalled to Germany without prior warning and summoned for personal interview by Hitler. His regiment were both surprised and mystified – and they are still mystified to this day as to the reason, knowing only that it was not a favourable one. Of course the Führer may have been in a passion over the disastrous ending to this last battle, though other heads were at stake then and far more important ones than Koch's. There may have been other reasons, but whatever they were Koch's soldiers were sad enough about it. They had been a long time together.

Walter Koch died on 27 October 1943, the brief report saying that he had met his end near Breslau – in a motor car . . . and so did Generalfeldmarschall Erwin Rommel barely a year later. But offending the Emperor is death however it comes.

Major Schirmer succeeded to the command of the 5th Paras. Like Koch he had been with them since the onset in France and the Low Countries in 1940, and in the opinion of Obergefreiter Preussner he was regarded with a respect not much different to that of his late chief.

Writing at this time to my mother:

"We are now leading a more peaceful life after a variety of excitements and a generally interesting time. We are in the best position now that we have had since the campaign started, and occupy some old ruins – Roman. . . . It is amazing how the work of those days still stands. It is mainly of hewn rock of immense proportions. . . . There is a lot of exquisite carving and I suppose it dates from Hannibal and Scipio Africanus 2500 years ago.

"The pièce de résistance here is a hot spring that throws up beautifully clear, and warm, water, so bathing is proceeding apace. We have a bath hewn out of stone by some ancient – eight foot long and two deep, and carved all round the sides – so I may be bathing in the same bath that Hannibal once used. . . .

"Have a new officer, Sillem, a type we badly need . . . but I have lost poor Dudley Clark who we had to evacuate. We have a delightful French dog named Roger who lives with us now. He is very popular and quite fearless. He has his own hole to get in to, which he does as soon as things get noisy and he doesn't mind a bit.

"I have discovered a weakness in my driver Quinlan. This part of the country is full of tortoises and the other day I found a tin full of leaves in the front of the truck, and in it a tortoise about the size of a crown piece. Asking Quinlan why he had become so motherly he said he thought it too young to be running about by itself.

"... Last night the Jerries were rude for a short while, but ineffectively so. Otherwise everything is very peaceful, and today is like spring, so will have another dip in my Roman bath if the sun stays out. . . ".

And to my father:

"By the way, Mum accidentally included in the notepaper she sent me, four 2d. stamps, various shopping lists, and some jam recipes. I thought she might need the latter so here it is. Could not send the original as had already written out a directive to the warriors on the back.

"... Save some port for us. The old cellar must be getting at low ebb by now. . . ."

On 22 March we pulled out of Grandstand for the last time, and moved north to Beja. The Inniskillings had already gone to this part of the 78th Division concentration area, where both regiments were to array themselves for their star parts in the drama ahead of us.

I will not forget Grandstand, nor the sinister silhouette of Djebel Rihane behind us, which in my memory at least was never to be overprinted until we came to Cassino. However on this night the usual black outline was blotted out in the darkest of nights as we headed across country to Djelida to our transport.

Our withdrawal was tense enough, and I had to rely on my compass for the six-mile march back, praying that we kept clear of minefields. Our divisional transport was responsible for lifting us, but coming to Djelida they had miscarried somewhat. These operations were usually testing. With an open front and close to the opposition anything could happen. However at length they appeared out of the darkness and we got our men in.

D Company slept for the rest of the night – for the first time for months – while these R.A.S.C. buses groped their way northwards.

The dawn had come by the time we reached Beja, where we were greeted by Mac and the colour sergeant. They had not only found billets, but Dave Bartlett and Corporal Strainger had also produced an exceptional breakfast, including bread, the first time I had seen it for months. I was always touched by this kind of welcome, sensing their thoughts, and knowing their devotion. I knew also that they had not slept that night, even if the rest of us had.

We did not stay long at Beja, and were there for only a few days. We used the time for zeroing all our weapons and in instruction by our sappers in the latest German mining techniques.

These anti-personnel mines were bestial weapons, and in my opinion were a perfect example of the Hun way of thinking. Like the cutting down of the apple trees in Picardy they gratified their feelings of hate. These A.P. mines served no military purpose that I knew, though they caused distressing casualties. They never stopped an attack, nor even a patrol, in our experience.

The A.P. mine was a thing like a large size jam jar within a jam jar. The inner canister was packed with musket balls and a small charge. The outer had a propellant at its base, the whole being set in motion by a three-pronged spike at the top, which actuated cap and fuse in the same way as one of our grenades.

The prongs of the spikes were the size of pins and these beastly contrivances, sunk in the ground, were virtually invisible. Certainly so at night. The enemy habit was to set them at lethal distance apart, that is about twenty-five yards, and string them together with piano wire the thickness of cotton.

On contact the canister simply was blown about ten feet into the air where it exploded, and one's chance of survival was fifty per cent, depending on which way the thing had tipped at the moment of the explosion.

Admittedly we became keener on daylight activities in the next phase, but we soon learned to look for these things. Sensitive as the A.Ps. were I have little doubt that the enemy killed their own people often enough when setting them. The best defence was to avoid the obvious approach routes where they were likely to be used.

At Beja we were made up to strength with two drafts, so the thoughts in the minds of our chiefs became obvious. These men were mainly from Warwickshire or Stafford, and we never had better. About thirty in all, they filled most of our gaps, and in Beja's placid surroundings we could at least make them feel at home.

We could not have had a nicer or more intelligent lot, and there was none of that tension that sometimes arrives with a new draft. I think they infused something into us. Perhaps it was the infectious enthusiasm which they brought with them. New blood, it was welcome among our case-hardened team. Easy and willing they were perfectly adapted to an Irish regiment, and personally I was glad to have them from the source they came from. Their solid Midland qualities imparted an element of stability among our mercurial Irish warriors, whose temperament sometimes needed some counterbalance. This was a very good mix indeed. The newcomers were an unemotional bunch, some said, but perhaps it was just as well.

As time passed, the Irish Brigade worked its magic upon them and cast its mantle around them. Nor was this long in happening, when only days remained before they found themselves embattled beside us. In spite of their origins they became fully identified with us, and a part of the Irish saga. And for those who survived, the regiment became their whole life for a while, and the background to it for ever afterwards.

Lieutenant Jack Chapman joined us here. Jack was an ideal counterpart to Peter. Intelligent and articulate, he also wore that negligent pose affected by cavalry subalterns and perfected by Dizzy Gethin. He was a very entertaining addition and an effective foil to the flamboyant Peter Sillem, who would have been the perfect model for Rembrandt's *Cavalier*. I posted Jack to 17 Platoon, thinking it would do them good to have this lithe and youthful character to set them alight after Martin's long reign.

Then Alec Smith came. Alec was another equally cheerful and robust character, though hardly out of the egg. His youthful enthusiasm would carry all before him, but to make sure that it did not take him too rapidly I put him with Chalky White. Fred White would hang on to his coat tails to hold him back when he became too adventurous.

These three subalterns of D Company, all aged about twenty, made me feel that matters might take some controlling – if they wanted to go faster and farther than I did. But I was becoming cautious in my old age, and now twenty-seven was feeling distinctly fatherly towards them.

We were now at our full strength.

The following night Beauchamp, Dick Jefferies and I went to the local sulphur baths for purification, but I cannot recall afterwards that we felt any the better for it.

We ended our stay with a cocktail party that went on for most of the night, and at its conclusion we could say that the new boys were fully assimilated. Hugh Holmes came in from corps headquarters, and Nick and Desmond of course from their companies. There were only two categories of drink – whisky and rum, both with additives. We celebrated Brandon's M.M., but it was a pity that he could not be there, and we should miss him in the days ahead.

On Saturday 3 April Beauchamp summoned me with the other company commanders and briefed us on the tasks confronting the Irish Brigade. The 78th Division was required to force open the road from Beja to Tebourba, and this could only be done by the seizure of the mountain barrier which dominated the whole of it. We in fact had to break down the portcullis of the Tunisian fortress and nothing else could happen until we had done so. Once that barrier was sundered an unrestricted armoured assault would carry all before it.

Our army was going over to the attack.

. . . And then the mules. None of D Company had ever seen one before, and the thought of our warriors actually taking over whole troops of these beasts hardly bore contemplation. They were heavy-handed enough with our trucks, and I could not conceive how they would fare with these fractious four-legged children of Satan.

An uninspiring French officer of the *déclassé* variety paid us a call with a view to instructing us in the art of living with the mules. As he could hardly speak any English and was virtually incapable of instructing anyone anyway, the lecture was not a success. In any case it was a waste of time talking until the moment came when we were actually confronted by the animals. Then the muleteers would take over, and demonstrate. Only then did I learn that our Irish warriors, and most of the others too, were quite at their ease with these horrible creatures.

It was a sobering thought when one realised that all our past training was based on supply by vehicles of one kind or another. No one thought of mountains in our peace-time training, but for the rest of the war we lived in them for the most part, and use and abuse of mules became habitual. We could neither have lived nor fought without them.

Though nothing could ever persuade me to like these beasts, I can understand their immense military value over the centuries. Indifferent both to danger and fatigue, their battle performance was extraordinary. It was a pity they were so bloody-minded.

On the Sunday morning our orders arrived and we now knew exactly what was expected of us. Our first onslaught at least seemed a fairly straightforward one, though we revised our thoughts later.

Mac with the other members of my administrative team had gone on ahead. Before the dusk came down I was on the march with D Company, heading for Oued Zarga and the mountains, thinking my thoughts which were absorbed by purely material problems, and how our soldiers would fare when confronted with thirty mules to load with ammunition at first light the following morning. They had never seen one yet.

Our piper, Green, pounded away at our head with "Jackets Green", "O'Neill's War March", and whatever else came in to his head as we marched a hundred strong over those rolling Tunisian folds. Perhaps Nelson Russell was right. It was not a bad country – the flat parts. Green ran out of puff as we worked up the foothills, but he had not done badly. He had been playing incessantly for the last ten miles. It had been a pleasant march in that cloudless evening, with scarcely a breath of wind, but there was a glinting haze which hid the feet of those mountains from us. That haze would cause problems, but whether for us or for the other side I knew not.

We reached our forward concentration area in the Munchar hills by midnight, finding that Mac had everything ready as usual. The company had to do nothing further that night save to feed and doss down, and that they never had to be told to do.

The regiment of course would do what was expected of it. It always had. Nelson knew that. However in other quarters matters were not so certain. The Faughs still relied on themselves alone, and their Inniskilling brothers beside them. They regarded other regiments with reservation then, and after their experiences so far in Tunisia they saw no reason either to modify their views or abate their own self-confidence.

PLATE 9

Bettiour. The O.P. Battle of Djebel Ang, 15 April 1943. All ground visible is held by the enemy. Heidous is mainly hidden in the folds of the middle distance, and beyond lies Djebel Tangoucha under bombardment. Forward left runs the long spur of Kef el Tior awaiting assault that night, with Point 622 hidden in the murk in the far background.

PLATE 10
Djebel Bettiour, base of that cliff which alone gave shelter, 15 April 1943.

9

The First Barrier

Djebel el Mahdi

THE MORNING WAS pleasantly idle and we had little to do as the mules were twelve hours late, with the result that everything hung fire while we waited for them. Delays and troubles of this kind I soon discovered to be common enough where mules were involved.

Beauchamp was not able to summon us until 7 p.m. to give out his orders. He had spent most of the day with the brigadier, and Nelson had been pushed around a good bit by his worried chiefs. The mules arrived at about the same time that Beauchamp sent for me, so I was spared the necessity of being present at the loading ceremony, which anyway would have been carried out far more efficiently by Dave Bartlett and the C.S.M. in my absence.

Strangely enough our fusiliers, once confronted with the unusual, responded to the novelty and got on with it. Coming back at the end and observing the scene of animals practising handstands and buck jumping, and our warriors flying when they did so, I wrote down that it ought to have been filmed. However by nightfall they had loaded up thirty-odd mules with small arms ammunition, the reserve Bren magazines, grenades, 2″ mortars, H.E. bombs, picks, shovels, and rations for the next forty-eight hours – and much else. It was no mean achievement, and after this traumatic experience I would recommend loading and controlling mules as a fit subject for infantry training, indeed an essential one, and preferably practised at night.

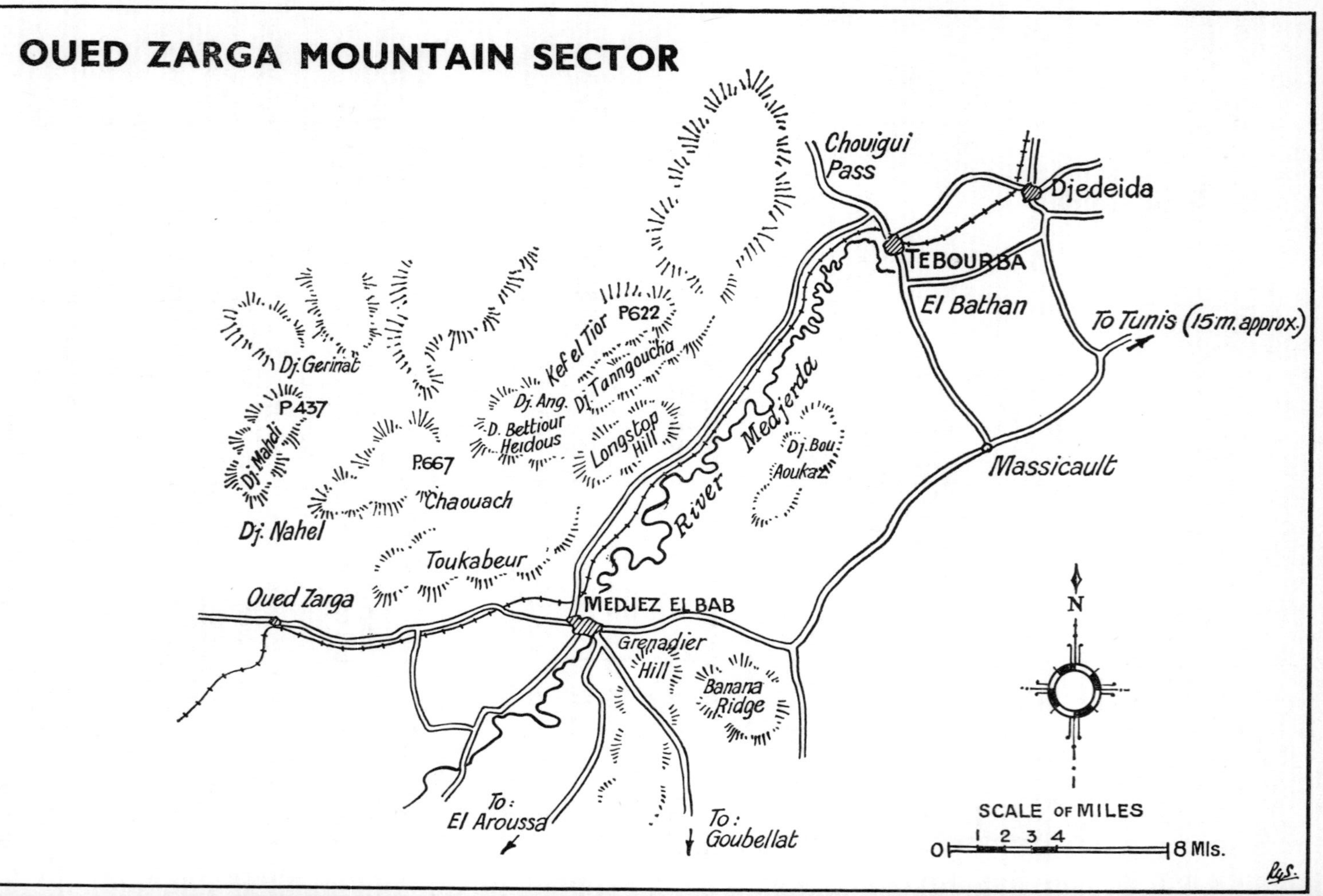
OUED ZARGA MOUNTAIN SECTOR
Chouigui Pass
Djedeida
TEBOURBA
El Bathan
To Tunis (15 m. approx.)
Dj. Gerinat
Kef el Tior
P622
Dj. Tanngoucha
Dj. Ang.
D. Bettiour
Heidous
Longstop Hill
River Medjerda
Dj. Bou Aoukaz
Massicault
P437
Dj. Mahdi
P.667
Chaouach
Dj. Nahel
Toukabeur
Oued Zarga
MEDJEZ EL BAB
Grenadier Hill
Banana Ridge
N
To: El Aroussa
To: Goubellat
SCALE OF MILES
0 1 2 3 4 8 Mls.

I put Jack Chapman in charge of the mule column. He looked as though he had spent most of his life in the saddle and was therefore the natural choice.

The night march through the hills was a bad one, and it was largely our own fault. None of the essential preliminaries had been properly carried out, and when one considers that a whole infantry battalion, with at least a hundred mules in train, was carrying out a night approach march to within small arms range of the enemy forward defences, it seems that we were leaving a good deal to chance.

There was probably some staff mis-timing in the beginning, but one delay breeds others, and after the late orders and the half day lost over the mules, the delicate operation in front of us was rushed quite unnecessarily.

As a result the battalion column, mules and all, got thoroughly mixed up during the night, and finally we became dispersed and lost.

Dispensing with the services of the intelligence section guides we then found our own way and arrived in in the daylight. We were not very clever that night and our intelligence officer, Jack Pierce, was rather upset, but in fact we were all to blame and had neither appreciated the problems nor reconnoitred the route. These were elementary enough matters but we had been pushing our luck, a fault which the Faughs were by no means immune to. Thereafter any officer knew that getting from A to B in the blackest of nights was his responsibility and his alone.

Jack learned the lesson the hard way with his thirty mutinous mules. He arrived with the animals two hours late and considerably vexed. He had discovered that mules had an infinite capacity for mischief, and several had tipped their loads overboard. Later our men would often abandon lost loads where recovery or tarrying were alike hazardous, but Jack regarded his honour as pledged and spent anxious and fruitless hours in salvage. He said afterwards that this was the worst night he had ever spent in his life so far, and it was also one of the rare occasions when D Company of the 1st Faughs had to wait for its breakfast.

The mountain slab of Djebel el Mahdi lay before us, though

still hidden from our sight save for its ugly top. Fourteen hundred feet high, this whale-shaped ridge was the first objective of the Irish Brigade. It lay as a barrier across the approaches to the higher and sharper-cut hills which stretched away eastwards in ever ascending array. Here the German positions had to be unhooked first, as an essential preliminary to dealing with the remainder.

The Inniskillings and ourselves were now lying concentrated at the mountain's approaches in a series of wadis ending in a narrow mile-long gorge.

We shared this uncomfortable rock-bound cleft with several hundred mules, and there were faint overtones of a day at the races, though the effect was spoiled by the unpleasant terrain around us. We were conscious of feeling crowded, and I am thankful indeed that we were unnoticed by the Stukas during that long drawn day. We would have been a dive-bomber pilot's dream. For some reason too the enemy just beyond us stayed as quiet as mice, and they cannot have known what was happening so close to their own front door. But they should have known had they been vigilant. These troops, hangers-on of Von Manteuffel's division on the northern sector, were recently raised units, and although temporarily stiffened by some of Oberst Weber's grenadiers were hardly in the same class as Koch's Jägers.

This gorge, in which we lay up for that endless day, was very steep-to, and facing south the thing was a suntrap. With the cliffs focussing the heat upon us we felt the first intensity of the African summer, and I thought of the Foreign Legion.

Here we stayed silent, all movement forbidden, and the day seemed to go on for ever.

The topography had the shape of a claret bottle with ourselves in the long neck, and the bottle being the mountain. The hill itself, four miles in length and a half of that wide, was known to be heavily defended and also thick with mines.

At the end of the neck, like a driven-in cork, lay the enemy forward defences. The position was a strong one and long prepared – and it effectively blocked that defile. Its weaknesses showed up later and, rare for Tunisia, the mountain's width and convexity made flank support difficult for the Germans. For much of its length the top was out of view from flanking features, and once safely up there one was visible only along the crests of the ridge itself, and from the sky. These advantages did not apply at the ends.

The Inniskillings, the 27th Foot, were the senior regiment, and naturally had the honour of leading the assault. Their orders were to unstop the bottle and, clearing the way for us, allow the Faughs to capture the rest of the mountain.

Apart from the heat we had a pleasantly restful day. We spent part of it discussing our battle tactics, and if there was any underlying tension I certainly never noticed it, though we remembered what had happened to the German attacks and thought that we would probably do better. In my spare time I read "The Life of Nelson" – of Horatio that is, our famous sailor having little in common with our rugged brigadier, save in serviceability and valour. I have often thought of that tale and would commend it to anyone facing trouble. I know of no better stimulant to one's motives.

The Skins were attacking that night, with ourselves following through them in daylight afterwards. So it was hoped, but all depended on the initial success of the Inniskillings in breaking in and clearing our base line. With their usual foresight and thoroughness they had had a good look round the foot of the Djebel before daylight that morning. Unfortunately when probing about in the wadis which intersected the approaches they ran into A.P. minefields and lost some of their men, but they found out what mattered and could warn the rest of the regiment – and they did not fail to let us know too.

As usual our senior regiment set about its task with complete absence of fuss, and the Inniskilling assault went in at midnight under a concentration of a hundred and fifty guns. By dawn they had succeeded entirely, they had shattered their opponents and held the whole of the southern end of the mountain.

Their C.O., Allen, died in the attack. Known in his regiment as "Heaver" he was a typical dogged Inniskilling, and they all liked him, as we did. His conduct was absolutely true to form. When one of his companies came under Spandau fire as they were crossing those wadis, Heaver felt obliged to deal with the problem personally – and so paid a soldier's forfeit. The Skins, like most regiments, responded to that kind of leadership.

Then it was our turn.

D Company breakfasted handsomely and early, but it was 10 a.m. before the Skins were in a fit state to receive us.

We set off down the cleft in single extended file and had hardly started before the enemy artillery opened up on us, using mediums again for the most part. Their fire was very unpleasant, but fortunately it was not coming down accurately on what should have been a pre-arranged and carefully registered target. We were well dispersed anyway, but I am glad that the shells fell mostly either beyond us or above, on the rocky tops of this extraordinary gorge we were moving down. As we proceeded, a steady shower of fragmented rock descended around us, bouncing and clattering down the cliff faces, from these hideous explosions going on overhead.

Before we emerged from the torment we were set upon by a troop of Messerschmitts who streaked down the gorge, firing their cannon and turning the place into a screaming madhouse, the general din reaching a crescendo as some nearby Bofors let drive into the rapidly vanishing aircraft. However the Messerschmitts achieved nothing other than upsetting a few of the mules who were plodding along in the rear with the sergeant major. These creatures would shortly be taking an active part in the forthcoming assault.

After about half a mile we emerged from the gloomy shadows of the gorge in to very different scenery. As the Germans were still firing industriously into the defile well behind us now, the tension eased considerably, and we could start to take an interest in our new surroundings.

Here the footings of Djebel el Mahdi rose sharply out of the ground in front of us and, end on to us, the mountain looked like a colossal plum pudding that had subsided rather badly. It was also much the same colour as one, black and brown and unspeakably ugly. The Djebel bore little sign of its overnight battle, but the wadi in front of us told its tale, leaving nothing to the imagination. That scrub thorn was very much in evidence, and unpleasant to move through it provided cover for nothing – save minefields.

Round the front edge of the slopes facing us was a prehistoric wadi bed carved out of the ground like some scouring of the last ice age. The thing was at least fifty yards wide with vertical sides to it, though these edges were sufficiently broken to enable one to scramble up it in places. The whole set-up only needed the glacis and the covered way to equate the best laid out "barrier" fortresses of the eighteenth century. The enemy had naturally selected their vast ready-made moat for their anti-personnel minefields.

The Inniskillings must have had a very rough time getting clear of the cleft like we were doing now, and deploying into their line of battle along the wadi's edge prior to their assault. Apart from the formidable natural obstacle in front of them the enemy picket line was scarcely a hundred yards off.

In spite of their previous night's reconnaissance, I do not think that the Skins knew the full extent of those minefields and we immediately discovered that we were heading through them ourselves. However there were a good many gaps, and the Skins had taped some of them. Elsewhere their presence was marked all too conclusively by Inniskilling dead, for our brother regiment had gone straight in over the top of them without pausing.

We ourselves were not in a hurry, being in fact ahead of the timings arranged in the brigade plan of battle. So we stopped for a while in the wadi and disarmed as many of the mines as we could see in the immediate vicinity. There was no difficulty about this as the pins were mostly still attached to them. Quite a number had already discharged and there was trailing piano wire all over the place. They may have caused casualties, but there was clearly not the slightest check to the Inniskilling attack. I noticed that a number of the canisters had never been armed, and we found this evident inefficiency comforting. Perhaps our opponents would fail in other ways too.

After this relaxation we hauled each other up over the bank of the wadi, wondering how on earth the Skins had been able to do it with the enemy sitting there on the top of it. That was just the kind of obstruction where a night attack could get completely out of hand in the face of a resolute enemy. I never discovered how Fred Fincham got the mules up when coming along behind us – but he did.

The Germans could not see our arrival but it was fortunate that their shelling was not more accurate in those confined approaches. D Company was vulnerable enough until clear of the wadi, but once safely on to the edge of the hill face there was no further bother, and we went forward in to the hard-won Inniskilling positions where we were greeted affectionately by our kinsmen. We could compliment them too on their night's achievements, for the Skins had the hardest part of this battle, and they set a standard which would carry on through, with both regiments, for the rest of the campaign.

Desmond Gethin followed with C Company, and we drew out our line of battle beneath the false crests ahead of us. The Inniskilling forward positions lay just under the ridges with the sentries concealed on the tops. They were just lying up there quietly, mostly half dug in. It was one of those strange periods of lull, and there was not much firing – just an occasional machine gun burst and the odd rifle shot, which was surprising with the enemy there in strength and so close in on us.

Desmond and I now put into effect the simple plans which we had concerted together the previous afternoon. He took C Company across the feature and lined out on D Company's left. Both companies had one platoon forward with the other two laid back on the flanks, and Desmond and I both stayed within reach of each other on the inner flanks so that we could control the battle together.

To start with Nelson had to his hand the whole of the divisional artillery and a number of medium and heavy regiments as well, but in practice, for this kind of battle, the army system of control was so perfect that in emergency any gun on the whole army front could be called into action from a single O.P. – providing it was within range and that the trajectory of its shells could clear the intervening mountain peaks.

At noon on 7 April 1943 all this supporting artillery went into action, and the crest line four hundred yards in front of us disappeared under the tornado of fire and steel which smote upon it. Erupting into an ever increasing grey-black cumulus, shot through with orange flashes and the continuous flickering flame of lightning, the maelstrom gradually spread itself outwards and skywards until it blotted out all forward vision – and hearing too for that matter.

It was difficult to believe that any of the opposition could have been left to fight when the firestorm ended.

Minutes passed. Then our gunners lifted their sights on to the main enemy positions on the higher ground – and repeated the treatment while we scampered forward to deal with the first targets before their occupants came to their senses.

We advanced using my preferred method of attacking with fire rather than by putting our men straight over the open. To that end the two flank platoons covered the third one forward in progressive hops from one false crest line to the next, sweeping the ridges with fire and shooting out the opposition until the attack went home. Only in one case did the enemy wait for us, but the sight of Alec and 16 Platoon charging in on them was too much for their nerves and they put up their hands.

Matters went fast enough and within three hours the whole mountain was in our hands.

As we advanced the enemy gunners opened with their defensive fire all over the place, but they could not see much and we were exceedingly lucky as most of the shelling fell behind us. They may have been firing blind, but the German artillery was badly co-ordinated at this stage of the battle ; ill-directed and too late, it was largely ineffective and their O.P. parties on the Djebel had failed them – but they may have been dead by then . . . or bolted.

Their other minions on the hill, their luckless infantry, also in many cases left matters too late. Being neither brave enough nor clever, they kept their heads down until there was no time left to them to do much about it – and we were protected by the curvature of the ground from M.G. fire from their friends on their flanks, a hazard which has wrecked so many attacks.

Reaching the end of the ridge was the climax. As we closed on our objective, almost at the last minute, the enemy garrison upped and bolted to a man, and I know of no experience in life remotely comparable. The sense and the emotive feelings of triumph with a flying enemy before one are like nothing I have known on any other occasion in this world. They were not far off, and every single one of them was running like mad, as fast as a man could run across such a broken countryside. A few of them dropped as our men settled down for some steady target practice, and the others gradually dispersed as they receded into the middle distance. Others just dived for cover as our Brens searched after them, and they did not reappear until later, when they were quite certain we had lost interest in them. Beyond doubt we had routed our enemy.

For a few minutes I lay down with my rifle and engaged the attractive series of targets in front of me racing over the hillside. Then I remembered that I was a company commander, indeed the force commander, and that "holy" Henry, Sid Smith 05, and others beside me were also marksmen and could shoot as well as I could. Leaving them to it I walked across to Desmond and we exchanged mutual expressions of esteem, waved at our victorious and grinning fusiliers, and concerted our next moves.

"Come triumph or disaster before the day be done." The poet actually wrote "glory" but he meant triumph, otherwise those words from the Harrow song book are meaningless. However they have always rung in my mind in extreme situations, and they did so now on Point 437 of Djebel el Mahdi. We had by no means won our battle yet and there could easily be triumph AND disaster.

We had reached our objective and we had flattened the opposition – part of it, but sloping away in front of us was the mile-long northern spur of the Djebel still apparently crawling with Hun soldiery. Admittedly they had had the mortifying experience of watching their own soldiers in panic flight before us as we carried the summit, but we had seen that too with our own men at the second Battle of Bou Arada, and we had still won our battle then, strategically anyway. The enemy in front of us on the northern end of the ridge were still not only intact but had not even been fired on by our guns. This had got to be dealt with immediately, otherwise they would be in to us at nightfall without wasting a moment. The Germans could be relied upon to show their usual resilience with an infinite capacity for mischief, and certainly this team in front of us should be left in no doubt of our intentions towards them, nor given time to recover from their present mortification. We must set upon them without further delay.

In our war, and in others throughout recorded history, the period of maximum danger is that following successful assault, when disarray and confusion temporarily confound the victors.

This was the historic moment when battles were irrevocably lost, when the impetus of the attack has faded and effective defence becomes the paramount need.

This situation was also the acid test of disciplined troops – getting the M.Gs. into well-sited fire positions and mutually supporting, refilling magazines, digging in and probing forwards and outwards with fighting patrols, posting the standing pickets – and registering the defensive fire tasks of the guns. That fire curtain might well be decisive, and the whole defensive tap would need to turn on at the flick of a finger as soon as night had fallen. No relaxation was ever possible, not until that first night was through and done with, and the enemy reaction known.

Our persevering gunners, the O.P. party, never left me, and they hung on my heels like a pair of gundogs, with their spare signallers and other acolytes trailing along in the immediate wake of the attack. They had even been first on the objective in one of their Tunisian battles. 132 Field Regiment were in our care for this one, or more truly we were in theirs, and their guns were now following our fleeing enemy and pounding away at them as they had done all day wherever they disclosed themselves. In this period the usual practice was for battery captains to accompany the spearhead of the attack, with their signallers beside them, and their battle technique was so well organised that they could call instantly on massive help in our moments of crisis – so long as they stayed alive.

My cousin James Browne was one of the ornaments of 132 Field Regiment, and he was a battery captain.

Quite a number of our retreating opponents seemed to have recovered their courage on the slopes in front of us. The other two platoons were still firing away hard at them and I sent Jack Chapman on with 17 Platoon to round up what he could, thinking that these men would throw in the towel when he reached them. In the meantime we covered him forward. Desmond was carrying out a similar sweeping-up operation with some of his own men, but below and beyond us the opposition was both numerous and excited, and far too much for us to cope with.

At this stage the Irish Brigade had pierced the enemy front deeply – four or more miles deep, but in other places, and especially on our eastern flank, the opposition was intact, and they could have destroyed us if we failed to contain them. In the meantime we were through to their gun lines, and the next thing I knew was that one of their self-propelled monstrosities was engaging us from across the draw below us over open sights. Then several others joined in, and they were momentarily beyond our reach.

Our gunners in their O.P. beside me were personally interested in this one, as they were the target too, but as we consulted I had the reply, "Sorry, old boy, it's on the list. We will be as quick as we can." The fact is that at the moment of victory they had far too many targets on every side, and who could say which of them mattered the most.

By the time 132 Field Regiment were ready that S.P. had pitched several dozen shells in to us and had caused us more vexation than the rest of the German artillery put together that day. It was all too personal. One could even see the flash of the damn thing firing, and could count the seconds until its projectile landed with the smashing roar of the explosion, half burying us in the process. Fortunately the top of the Djebel was a soft one, and one could burrow quicker than usual.

At length our gunners began to range upon our persecutor from our O.P., having called up a battery of mediums for the purpose. To begin with they were disappointingly wide, but in a few minutes the colossal bursts of these 5.5s. began to creep towards the S.Ps. Then they began pitching alongside. And then silence as black clouds of ever increasing smoke hid the scene from us, a mute picture of utter desolation like the rest of the slopes around. The German guns remained silent afterwards.

That out of the way, Fincham arrived with the mules, with our mortar ammunition, the spare Bren magazines, and all the other necessities of life. Beauchamp also sent forward a section of Vickers guns, and while all this was in progress we experienced a sight that could never be forgotten.

The Germans may have been in doubt as to the progress of the battle during the period of the assault, but they could have been in none whatever by this time, and they had already turned most of their available weapons on to us. They now honoured us with the personal attention of a squadron of Stukas with a view to blasting us off their beastly hill, and we found them plunging down on us before we even knew of their presence.

The Stukas arrived simultaneously with a number of Spitfires, and the ensuing combat was fought out at deck level in a shattering crescendo of aircraft cannon, bombs and exploding aircraft, the like of which those valleys could never have heard before – nor ever would again.

One of the Stukas never pulled out of its dive, and went straight into the ground at full throttle like a streaking fire ball. Others caught by our pilots at the moment of pulling out were burning fiercely and went down in the nearby hills, the black palls of smoke rising up into the sky behind them like the explosions of their own aircraft bombs.

In the smoke and cloud and the evening murk I cannot think how our pilots could see to shoot, let alone fly their aircraft straight into the enemy among those mountain cud sides.

Jack came back with his platoon. He had nineteen prisoners but they had fought it out before they surrendered.

He and Robbie had fought a private battle of their own almost beyond our reach to help matters. 17 Platoon had run into and collected up a few scattered remnants – fugitives from our attack. But over a quarter of a mile in front of us they found themselves confronted by intact enemy forces concealed under the crest and well dug in. Both parties became aware of each other's presence at the same time and 17 Platoon sailed in to the attack, simply left-forming in extended line and charging up the hill without further ado. There was an intense fire fight as they did so, our warriors pausing only to fire from the shoulder as they went up, and using their Brens from the hip. They may have broken all the rules, but they wasted no time and the results were highly effective. Before 17 Platoon closed on their prey, the undamaged members of the garrison got to their feet with their hands up. Unfortunately they had shot most destructively first.

Jack had done well but he was severely wounded in the head and half blind, and he had several other casualties. He brought Fusilier Winston back with him – a pleasant lad but wounded to death with his leg almost off at the hip. Winston smiled cheerfully and appeared to be in no real pain. I said the nicest things I could think of to him and we shot him full of morphia. He could hardly have lived an hour or two.

We dug ourselves in and we thought our thoughts in the night that followed. We had lost twelve of our men, but there were over thirty enemy dead around us and probably a good many others on the hillside ahead of us. In addition to our battle casualties three of our men had run for it. New boys of course and they couldn't know.

We had won this battle anyway, but we lay the whole night behind our weapons with Alec Smith out beyond us to frustrate any Hun surprises. The night was an exceptionally cold one but David, the colour sergeant, had of course not failed us with our rum supplies.

Shooting and sniping went on for most of the night as the enemy probed around us, and at first light we turned the Vickers on to several groups of them apparently digging themselves in on the ridges opposite.

Then Beauchamp sent Nicolas forward and through us, with A Company, to tidy the front up. This they did rapidly and effectively, and returned with a further thirty-five prisoners. That made the regiment's total a hundred and twenty so far since the onset of the battle.

There had been an incident with the prisoners which both defied the imagination and illustrated perfectly the unpredictable make-up of some of our Irish warriors.

Fusilier Harry Fisher had charged up the hill with his comrades of 17 Platoon, and had come through that sharp little action unscathed. Harry in his pre-Hitler days had been a boxer of international standing. He was a regular soldier too, from Belfast, but this day he forgot the rules when Robbie unleashed him upon his disconsolate foes who had just thrown down their weapons. While Harry under Robbie's supervision was searching and emptying out the pockets of the late enemy, with wounded and dying men around him, he suddenly recognised the flattened nose and cauliflower ears of a broken pugilist in the crestfallen ranks opposite—and under Robbie's horrified gaze he promptly embraced the fellow.

On 10 April we were relieved by the Black Watch, and were sent on with a squadron of the North Irish Horse to clear the rest of the northern spurs of the mountain and capture Djebel Gerinat, four miles ahead. This was no problem and there was scarcely any fighting, as the Germans considered it indefensible after the loss of their main positions and pulled out as soon as they saw our tanks.

We captured two of the opposition en route who had clearly got lost, or perhaps had gone to sleep and had not been noticed when their friends departed.

Perhaps over-confident now, we were not careful enough, and on arrival were heavily shelled by S.Ps. from a neighbouring ridge, maybe getting rid of their ammunition before departing. However they hit Corporal Millar and we lost another good N.C.O.

Our practices at night in these circumstances, when we were in close contact with the enemy, had been determined by experience. All our weapons were manned and our company mortars usually loaded with flares. The guns of our field regiment were lined up on their prearranged defensive targets so that the batteries themselves required only a whisper to go into action.

Our men at their posts lay behind their Brens with half the sections asleep beside them and a pile of spare magazines ready to hand; and we always loaded tracer, without which night firing is rarely effective.

There were no sentries as such, and "stand-to" at first light only concerned administration; not the ability to fight, for our men had to be ready to do that instantly at any time of the night. And at all times in battle we relied on our pickets to warn us. These were sometimes a quarter of a mile or more in front of us and often were actually patrolling around us.

Sitting on Djebel Gerinat I wrote home:

"My dearest Mum ... I am afraid it is some time since I last wrote. We have been busy since. . . . The bag has been a large one, so much so that we have been unable to offer proper hospitality and entertainment to our guests. . . .

"The warriors are now confident and cocky . . . and have developed a contempt for the opposing team (dangerous,

J.H.C.H.). . . . One only has to see the type of chap that Hitler is now using. Personally I have felt sorry for some of them. Poor little chaps – some of them haven't the least idea what they are fighting for, and care less. . . .

"It has been very gratifying to see the results of four years with D Company. I know that there are no better troops in this world than our regiment.

"I have not actually met James again but we have, as it were, felt his assistance and presence . . . nice being supported by one's family."

And to my father :

"It would not have suited you here. I think that the guns you had would have shot too flat to cope with the Tunisian mountains . . . today we have had a grand time washing socks and other clothes that are quite wonderfully filthy. . . .

"Our rations have improved and we have tried our friends' stocks – really nice butter and Bologna sausage made from bacon . . . They left quite a lot in their haste."

The Battle of Djebel el Mahdi did not excite the historians. It was hardly spectacular enough, and there was also the national habit of ignoring military operations which succeeded as planned. None the less it was a battle which had to be won, and had the result turned out differently the subsequent operations would hardly have been possible.

Less than justice has been done to the German defenders of that mountain, even by our regimental accounts. The enemy was not lacking in resolution, but they had no real chance. There has been some doubt as to who actually commanded, as Djebel Mahdi lay between two divisional fronts and there may have been divided authority. But however that may be they were not as well organised as usual, and they were poorly supported ; nevertheless had the brigade's attack been bungled there could well have been a very different outcome. There was just a hint of what they were capable of when their survivors rallied against Jack's men at the end of the attack.

We succeeded as the assault had been meticulously planned, and it was carried through swiftly to its conclusion without checks or

PLATE II

Generaloberst Jürgen von Arnim.
Commander in Chief of the German
Forces in Tunisia.

Photograph taken approx. 16 May 1943. Guest of the U.K.

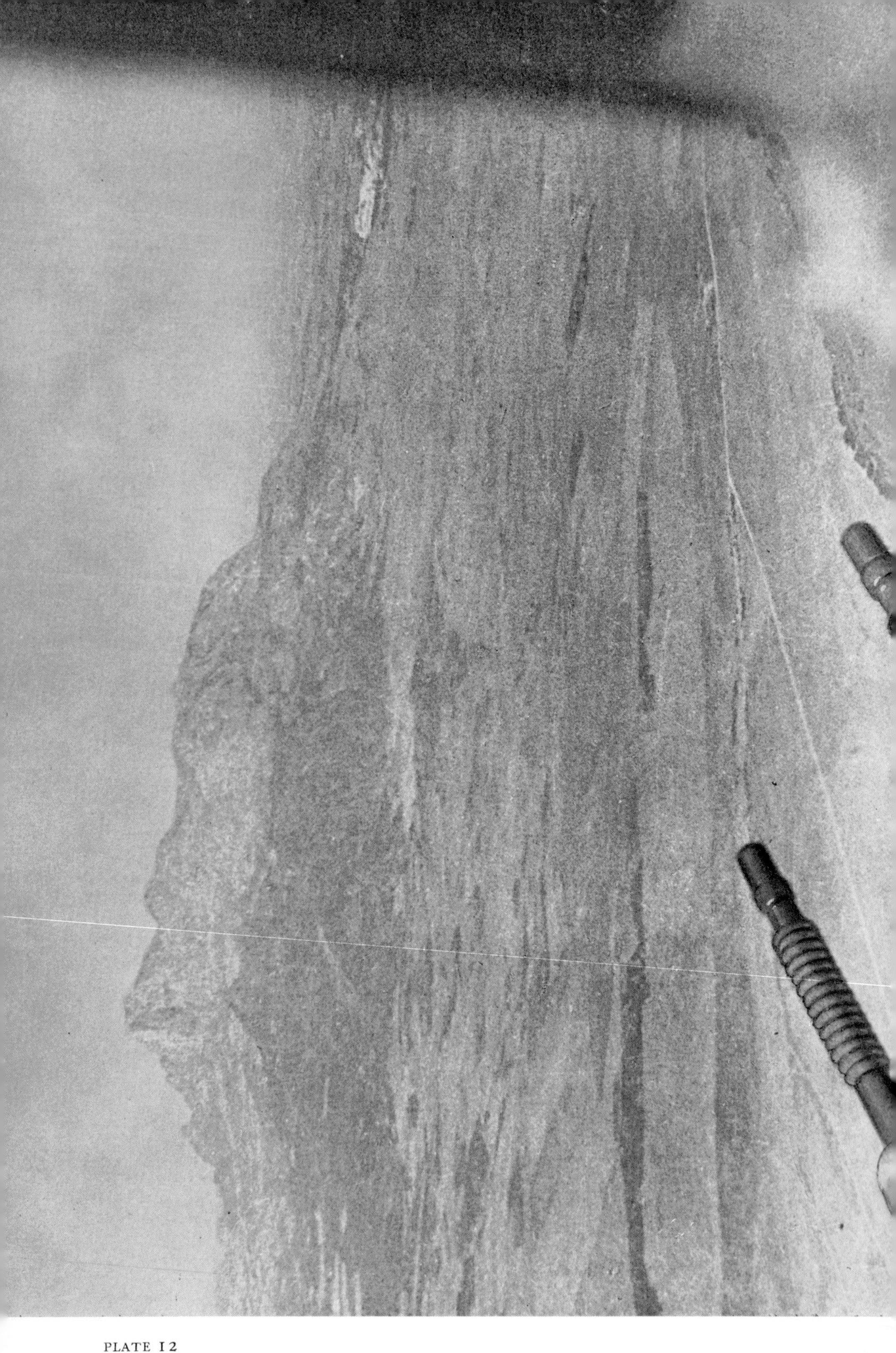

PLATE 12

Zaghouan massif, "whence came the wild geese". Photograph taken by Captain Michael Horsfall, from his Hurricane fighter bomber in action, April 1943.

serious mistakes. Also the Inniskillings and ourselves were at full strength – and fresh. In the battles that followed this was by no means the case, and fatigue, as well as losses, played a recognisable part in them. After this the cutting edge of the Irish Brigade sword was never quite so sharp – nor could it have been. It had been pretty thoroughly used in hacking our way through the first barrier.

10

Djebel Ang

THE FAUGHS PULLED out from Djebel Gerinat at dusk and moved back through the mountains – south and then east, marching twelve miles non-stop, as a preliminary move towards our new objectives.

We stopped at midnight and lay up for the whole of the following day beside Plateau farm ; christened thus by the 78th Division it had become quite well known. The farm lay just beside the gorge where we had begun the battle four days previously, and there the French patron and his numerous family were rounding up their livestock after living in no man's land for most of the winter. Recently they had entertained Inniskilling patrols and the local German mountain troops on successive nights – once on the same night, to the edification of both, according to Nelson Russell's pungent comments. Nelson also remarked that if anyone thought that a farmer's life was dull, this one never had a dull moment – not in our time anyway.

The Irish Brigade had been given one day's grace to rest and refurbish prior to moving across the divisional front from the western flank to the east where, on the right of the line, the 11 Brigade attack was in very serious trouble.

We occupied ourselves during that precious day in checking our weapons, replacing our ammunition, and sleeping, and at 5 a.m. on 13 April we were on the march for Chouach, over the mountains, carrying full ammunition scales. I recorded that it was a tough march, and the longest thirteen miles that I had ever known.

These marches are better understood in relation to the terrain. Toukabeur, Chouach, Kelbine and Heidous, the last just recaptured by the enemy, all lay in a row running eastwards, and they were mountain villages of a kind quite familiar to our army in its century-long warfare on the North West Frontier of India. Mostly perched high up on the rocks, and connected only by goat tracks, the term "marching" hardly does justice to the geography. This was in reality a scrambling cross-country trek along the sides of the mountains, and our sappers being busy with bulldozers on the goat tracks merely made matters worse. Toukabeur and Chouach had only been carried by 11 Brigade a few days previously, and the road-making for our vehicles was rapidly progressing as we moved, mules and all, through the opaque dust clouds.

Green still improved the situation with his pipes, even if he was lining both lungs and chanter equally with that fine ground grey talc hanging in the dewy morning air.

The following morning we lay up briefly in the olive groves on the top of Chouach massif and watched the Stukas dive-bombing our tanks down in the dips a thousand or more feet below us. Kendal Chavasse came to lunch with us during this last restful pause, that green beret of his scarcely doing justice to his usual patrician appearance, or to his complexion which, no doubt due to the African sun, had acquired the ruddy hue sometimes achieved in the Scottish Highlands – by the wintry winds and whisky.

Kendal commanded 78th Division's reconnaissance regiment, and being a Faugh himself lost no opportunity of paying his respects and dining with his brother officers. On our part we enjoyed both seeing him and knowing that one of our own kin was there as the eyes and ears of our own division. Kendal was a contemporary of Pat Scott, and we had spent endless days on the ranges together in those happy far-off days at Bordon, before Kendal's elevation to higher things.

Green of course performed for our distinguished visitor, and Dave Bartlett acquired a tablecloth from somewhere, so our lunch party was a suitably elegant prelude to the next part of the drama – though disturbed at intervals by our Bofors gunners who lost no opportunity of split second shooting at their pestilential opponents. The opposing airmen spent the whole morning whipping over and round those ridges and our persevering gunners had as much chance of hitting them as a blind man engaging driven snipe. Though we did not then know it I think we were witnessing the last fling of the Luftwaffe in North Africa and spectacular though it was they expended their remaining strength in their vain efforts that day.

Kendal was just about taking his leave when Beauchamp called the company commanders forward on to Djebel Bettiour, about three miles forward and eastwards of us. I left Mac with orders to bring the company forward an hour later, and to get our men in as near in to the Djebel as he safely could – and to feed the warriors when he got there in readiness for whatever adventures the forthcoming night held for us.

I went on ahead with Clanachan and another hectic bit of mountain climbing followed, taking us up a full two thousand feet further. As we scrambled up we found ourselves first in fog, which tanged unpleasantly with the sharp scent of explosives, but higher still we emerged into swirling clouds and mist banks like those of a highland autumn. The whole opaque scene was being thickened up by an unceasing rain of German mortar bombs spread wide over the landscape ahead of us. Finally we were above the fog level altogether, and from over the top of it we witnessed a scene only equalled in later times at Monte Cassino.

The view over the mist revealed a fairyland of white-crested ridges rising out of the cotton wool blanket beneath them. Wraith-like smoke hung over the nearby peaks and the whole surrounding scene was tormented by the red-black flashes of exploding shells and the shrieking scream of their flight. The orchestration was completed by the hysterical sounds of the Spandaus.

The enemy were fighting desperately with all this land disputed, and in a series of vicious counter attacks they had recovered most of it. All three battalions of 11 Brigade had suffered heavily in their initial set piece attacks on Djebel Ang, and the grim peaks beside it, and they had neither the men nor the means to hold them when the Germans hit back at them. There had been no withdrawal or any kind of rout – only the forward posts progressively surrounded and overcome, mostly during the night. Many of them had fought it out and simply vanished. As a result the individual companies of all three regiments of 11 Brigade were, most of them, down to a handful, and little further could be done for the time being, save to hold the springboard for ourselves.

The superb battlefield itself was sufficient to underline the vital issue being fought out across it, and I have no doubt that it deeply impressed the soldiers of both sides. It certainly did in my case and I expect it had its effect in the bitter resistance of the enemy. As beautiful as it was sinister, the picture before us only required the "Ride of the Valkyries" painting in overhead to complete the hellish scene.

In all these hills around us the only part that was firmly in our hands was the cliff face opposite. Bettiour, a square solid lump of a mountain forming the southern bastion of Djebel Ang which glowered at us over it, Ang's full three thousand feet rising majestically above its sullen and truncated neighbour.

We still held on to Bettiour, due only to the protection of that cliff face. The enemy were plastering it with their mortars, but the bombs that missed the lip of the feature went far over into the cud below, mostly among the mules struggling to bring the ammunition up.

And here on this lip edge of Bettiour, Beauchamp gave us his orders. Beside us lay our persevering gunners with their signallers and other tacksmen, hitting back hard at an endless series of targets. This had become a defensive battle.

". . . routs and discomfitures, rushes and rallies . . .", thus the bard in *Forty Years On*. Harrow could produce verses for all situations. I did not like discomfiture much, but I did not think there would be any rout, not as far as the 1st Faughs were concerned. But all this was here and the battle very far from won, and if we did anything stupid now it could be quite irrevocably lost.

Djebel Ang lay just over left, stormed the previous night by the Lancashire Fusiliers. The Surreys had taken over from them and were now trying desperately to hold it and, for that matter, Bettiour itself. But they were out of contact with their posts, and in the uncertainty and confusion defensive artillery fire was impossible.

Beauchamp spoke to us in his usual apologetic manner, and explained that we had been brought in to restore the battle which seemed to have turned against us. It could have been a mess discussion but for the madhouse around us. He pointed out that nothing could be taken for granted, and that he could not truthfully say that we held any of the ground about us save where we now stood, and not even the opposite lip of Bettiour two hundred yards off, across its flat and ugly table top which our adversaries seemed to be using as one of their principal aiming points. I hoped they would go on doing so. No one in their senses would go on top of the damn thing where there was no cover for a mouse, let alone a cat. We owed everything to ugly Bettiour and its weird fantastic profile. Bettiour would go on protecting us and we should regard with awe the local deities who planted this strange barrier in the path of our momentarily victorious enemy.

We used the remainder of the evening light in that superb O.P. trying to fix in our minds the features of the Grimm's fairy-tale landscape before us. Bettiour and Ang; then beyond Ang the ridge of Kef el Tior with its dragon's teeth top. Over right lay Djebel Tangoucha with the unpleasant, though well named, village of Heidous at its foot. Beyond again, and below, lay Longstop Hill. These were the mountain milestones of the road ahead. Strange names, but engraved for ever in the hearts of the soldiers of the 78th Division.

When I could see no longer I went back to the company, and before the night was ended we were miraculously established in the col, or saddle, which joined the flat top of Bettiour to Djebel Ang. We dug ourselves in faster than usual, and in the meantime Dave Bartlett had tucked the mules away safely under the cliff face now just below us. But they too had had their casualties.

Our colour sergeant and his men had had a rough time coming up the long draw behind Bettiour with the mules – and a slow business too, proceeding from one hole to the next, for the Germans were taking the obvious precaution of shelling the approaches. David had just about reached the foot of the cliff when Beauchamp and Dick Jefferies came racing down the thing in a showering, sliding cascade of scree. Their return from our conference at the top of it coincided with the arrival of a dozen or so 5.9s, and all three of them dived for cover into the same shell hole. The mules alas could not take cover, and suffered accordingly.

The fighting continued all night on Ang, and by the dawn we knew we had lost it to the enemy. The firing had never ceased and now their Spandaus were in action just above us. Further they could not come; not in daylight. We knew nothing of the fate of the Surrey defenders. They never came back through us, and by now they were either dead or in the hands of the enemy.

I went forward along the ridge to study our route of approach, for Ang was now our assignment, and this narrow neck in front of us made a nasty defile to take the company over once darkness had come – and I did not like that scree.

A Lancashire Fusilier subaltern lay there relaxed in death, revolver beside him, and a little beyond a dead officer of the enemy, the spent cases of his pistol scattered around him. True men, both of them.

Then I went back to the O.P. at Bettiour and picked up Nicolas, for Beauchamp had given us the honour of leading the assault that night. Ang was our objective, and Kef el Tior beyond it.

Nick was very subdued, quite unlike his usual self, and he seemed detached and withdrawn as we worked the thing out together. But he neglected nothing. We spent a long time there, mainly examining the ground through our field glasses. Sensing his attitude, and rather concerned, I asked Nick if anything was worrying him, knowing perfectly well that he feared nothing on this earth. But on this occasion he never told me the truth which he knew all too well during that last afternoon on Bettiour. He looked at me, silent and absolutely solemn, for quite a while. Then as we left to go back to our companies, Nick turned to me and said, "John, I am glad that we are doing this together." He also said something about having to tell me that.

Both companies had had a wretched enough day on the col under shell and mortar fire which had never ceased once. Well dug in, they were fairly secure, but we now noticed the phenomenon of shell shock for the first time, and a few of our men were slightly fuddled. They had been on their own for most of the day, thinking their thoughts and knowing nothing of what was happening. But they knew things were hideously wrong.

Their response was immediate once orders were issued. As Robbie once wisely observed, the officers and N.C.Os. were always fully occupied in the line and had little time for worry, but under our present circumstances our poor fusiliers had nothing to keep them going and only themselves to think of. These were the times which disclosed the latent strength of our army – the capacity for endurance and the meaning of comradeship. These were the intangibles which kept our soldiers together as they always had done in times of stress.

Beauchamp saw us again at 5.30 p.m. and gave the final orders for the night attack and the details of the fire plan. He actually came round to the company with these details, though there was little further to add other than the timings. I expect he had other reasons for wanting to see his companies, but he did not have to do any such thing. We as always were pleased to see him, and he had arrived in time for some rum. The last hour that remained to us afterwards was given over to our own arrangements for the attack, and to briefing Peter and Alec and the N.C.Os. Mac and the colour sergeant would bring forward all our necessities of life to sustain us as the battle ended, and they would probably arrive before it ended if I knew them truly.

The briefing done, it only remained to issue the rum ration to our ill-used warriors and, last thing of all, to deal with Lance Corporal Given.

By some extraordinary aberration 17 Platoon had failed to finish its rum ration, an error never known before nor likely ever to be repeated. It may have been due to a new N.C.O. with the company, Sergeant Morrisey, who was conducting the issue to 17 Platoon and who was perhaps unfamiliar with our practice in these matters. He was also clearly unfamiliar with Corporal Given's interests. However Robbie, now the platoon sergeant, knew all of these things, but his usual alertness failed him for once. He should have known better.

The vigilant Given noticed his chance and, spying the rum jar from afar beside his sergeant's kit, he homed on it in a flash, and thus entered his penultimate battle reduced to the ranks, in close arrest and quite wonderfully drunk.

It made little difference to his performance that night, and with greater matters afoot even his hangover passed unnoticed. He was promoted back again the following morning.

Thus we entered the Battle of Djebel Ang – the sublime and Corporal Given mixed together. But frivolous distractions had a way of creeping in to our more serious moments.

We took about seventy men into the assault on Djebel Ang, this figure excluding our mule teams. Moving off at last light over the scree and the ridge in single file we came on to Ang and lined out to our left. A Company followed and came in on our right, and during these tense minutes the enemy shelling was falling well beyond us.

At this stage we were relatively safe as we were no more than a hundred yards or so from the enemy pickets sitting up there in the scree just above us. Owing to the very sharp fall-away in the mountain side the enemy forward vision from those rocks could hardly have been more than a pistol shot, but we could not see them either. We just knew they were there. The principal advantage always in this situation is that neither side can use its artillery, and it is a historical fact that in our night assault on Djebel Ang the Faughs formed up their line of battle within comfortable shot-gun range of the enemy. We were not even particularly quiet as we did it, with our warriors slipping and sliding in that damnable loose rock, and falling over each other to boot. And even in tense moments like these they were inclined to be garrulous. Fortunately the enemy shelling screaming over our heads and dropping into the gorge behind us smothered most of our indiscretions.

As soon as the company had reached its positions we packed all the automatic weapons into our front rank, Brens slung from the shoulder into the hip position, and A Company did likewise. The rest of our men were lined back on our flanks, and Nick and I stayed together in the middle to keep the thing together. Somewhere in all these ranks behind me Fusilier James Given was firmly anchored to one of his comrades, minus a rifle and loaded to capacity with Bren magazines.

We then crept forward to our start line, and as we did so the Ang garrison opened up on us with their Spandaus. We just stopped and lay down and I think that the slight curvature of the hill top hid us from view.

At 7.30, our zero hour, the top of Ang and the Kefs beyond went up in smoke and flame under our barrage. As the flight line of the shells on to the 3000 foot mountain crest was scarcely above our heads, this close support was more personal than usual. Even so the forward enemy posts, being close to our start lines, were inside the line of the barrage and therefore immune. The brave men who manned them opened fire on us, but only momentarily for they were cut down very quickly under the packed fire of our eighteen Brens.

Then for the first time I heard the wild Irish yell of "Faugh a Ballagh" as our men stormed forward into the battle, their basic emotions stirred by I know not what. In a minute or two we had to bring the whole line to a stop to recover control of them before they got completely out of hand.

Ang was easy and we collected the rest of the garrison as the barrage passed over them. Some of them were picked up by Fred Fincham, coming along behind us with the ubiquitous mules.

Then our guns lifted and we moved on to the fantastic serrated saw-blade crest of Kef el Tior, and here the enemy artillery replied in kind. Here Nick was down, mortally wounded, and Phil Slattery his subaltern. No officers of ours had such a requiem as these two, with the echoes of our regiment's war cry following them to Valhalla. Nicolas would have thought of that as his life ebbed from him.

Once into the Kefs our fighting formation was no longer possible, and it became a matter of climbing and crawling over the bestial rocks. Fortunately there was no opposition worth counting after our guns had finished their task, though several times we suddenly found fuddled Germans in our midst, well past caring and only too glad to throw in the towel. Then we found Beauchamp among us, which was highly improper – our valuable C.O. certainly had no business at all in the front line of a night attack. Still, you can't change people.

The Kef ridge came to an abrupt end about a mile and a half from our start line, and here we paused to consider. Seemingly we had reached our objective, though this was far from clear in that lunar-like landscape with the mist coming down.

At this stage we could have gone right through to the German gun lines with nothing to stop us, but daylight would have ended that kind of adventure. What mattered now was to hold what we had won. Here we could do so on that flat end of the mountain where digging was possible. Moreover the sky line lay close in around us. We could see from that rim in the daylight, but the enemy could hardly see us.

The problem of resisting the enemy's counter measures was far greater after a night attack than ever it was in daylight, and in its way was the most critical part of the operation. This was shown all too clearly by 11 Brigade's experience over the self-same ground scarcely twenty-four hours earlier. There must be no repetition tonight, otherwise the 78th Division would have no one left to continue the fight and the mountain battle would be irretrievably lost. It is not just the loss of ground that matters when the assaulting force is wiped up by counter attack. There is the extremely destructive effect on the regiments who suffer this misfortune. That is the real loss and it cannot be overestimated for it is often decisive. But it also applies in reverse, and a shattered counter attack usually means the end of the force that undertook it and paralysis of all other resistance afterwards. The last flick of the battle is the most deadly part, the forfeits are at their highest, and we had just witnessed a vivid illustration of this truth – with the Irish Brigade hauled from one end of the front to the other as the sequel to it.

I spent some time inspecting that rim and trying to be sure of the fall of the ground. After a while I realised that it was rather like the other end of Ang itself – that is convex and blind where the feature terminated. I thought we could hold that top in safety, but there was a nasty thing sticking out in front like a bombed-out railway embankment. One could not really be sure of anything as the visibility worsened, and after a while it was well under a hundred yards; just a white opaqueness at the ground level. Overhead the stars were shining and the sky was bright enough. Also, the prow of the Kef was sticking up over the mist, silhouetted black against the night sky behind it.

Beauchamp in the meantime had been doing his own reconnaissance, but he came back shortly after seeing A Company into position in the craggy clefts just above us. A Company were now without officers, and Beauchamp said he would need Mike McDonald – and "hoped I wouldn't mind". Mac of course was the obvious choice and we sent back for him immediately. Desmond had also come up, and Beauchamp put C Company in on the other side of A, high up in the dragon's teeth but sufficiently far back to prevent us from being encircled, we hoped, when the daylight came.

The mist was becoming a good deal denser while Beauchamp and I were talking, and we both knew that the Germans would try their luck in it as soon as they knew what had happened.

We both noticed the strange unnatural silence around us, disturbed only by the clink of our men digging with their entrenching tools and the low voices of the N.C.Os. As we had just broken over a mile through the enemy defences, at their most critical point, we were slightly nonplussed, albeit thankful. The noises of battle seemed far away and below, seemingly thousands of feet below, on our southern flank and behind us.

Fincham arrived with the mules, and the colour sergeant – and tea. He and David had the mortars with them, and picks and spades which were vitally necessary in those rocks. They also brought all the rest of our heavy kit and the means to seize and hold what we had just captured. Our signallers set up shop, and then Tommy Wood, the battalion mortar officer, positioned himself on the rim and organised his minions against the morn. Tommy's task immediately became double-barrelled, as we sent him over to assist A Company until Mac could get his affairs sorted out.

About 5 a.m. we were joined by 132 Field Regiment – my cousin James Browne the battery captain with his O.P. party, and a pair of mules with their radio and other kit. They were dangerously late and had been held back on those narrow approaches at our tactical H.Q. while the rest of the battalion took up its positions. This was a mistake, and James did not have sufficient time to register his guns before the storm broke upon us.

Beauchamp sent us one of the Vickers sections, and I gave insufficient thought to their siting. It was no good trying to put down heavy machine guns in the black night and mist without knowing how the ground lay about us. One could take certain precautions like keeping close in to the sky line to avoid being overlooked, and above all by getting well dug in, but in this case the Vickers could not even do that due to the solid rock beneath them. As the mist thickened we could no longer see the sky lines. In the end we put them in among the rocks on the side of the spur where it would have been better sense to have hidden a sniper. At that stage we ought to have kept the Vickers behind us as backstops.

On our immediate right I knew that there was a fairly steep cliff down to Heidous, which lay about a thousand feet below us. On our right front sat the ugly hump of Djebel Tangoucha with its serrated top sticking out above the white mist carpet like a long-dead stranded whale with its ribs showing. Then, nearer in, two hundred yards off, lay a rocky projection like the overgrown battlements of a ruined castle. Straight in front the ground fell away sharply, but on our left, stretching away behind us, was the northern rampart of our position – the long vertebrae of the Kef el Tior spur, with its jagged crest line fifty or so feet above us. I hoped that it protected us, though I was not too sure. In the meantime the mist lay opaque on the ground, but above was the light sky and the stars and the first faint glow of the dawn.

We knew perfectly well during the last stages of the attack that we had entered a vacuum, though I could not deduce what was happening. However it was beyond reason that the enemy could have left so brittle a front on this vital feature.

During this phase we had been subconsciously aware of a very considerable battle in progress behind us but, engrossed in our own affairs, we could ignore other people's problems for the time being. Anyway we knew that the Inniskillings were attacking Tangoucha from the other side of Bettiour as the other half of the Irish Brigade's plan. The Skins' operations were not usually quiet ones, though there did seem to be a quite extraordinary amount of small arms fire going on below us as well as along the western sky lines in our rear.

What we did not then know was that the German garrison of Kef el Tior had launched a night attack on Bettiour at the same time as our own attack, and that the two teams had passed in the dark. So here we were on their home ground in the absence of most of the defenders.

It was of course an obvious German move and should have surprised nobody. The enemy had dispossessed us of the whole of 11 Brigade's winnings, save for the one key feature of Bettiour. He would hardly leave us with that one after his successes the previous night. And how could he know that the Irish Brigade would appear so smartly in the sector when they had last been seen on the other side of the front at Gerinat. Seizure of Bettiour was the final stroke left to the Germans to restore their battered front, and it was lunging at the heart of the 78th Division's attack at the same time. But they denuded their other positions to do it, and as in most gambles the winner took all.

In the meantime the defence of Bettiour was conducted by a mixed bag of mule teams and gunners, quartermasters and cooks, and the Irish Brigade headquarters. This was a soldier's battle fought out with grenades and small arms at point blank range on the frightening edge of that cliff. Here the casualties were to fall a hundred or more feet down the scree, and here, as the Germans closed, the battle went completely out of control, and they became so inextricably mixed with the garrison that for a while both sides were shooting indiscriminately into each other. Under these circumstances the advantage lay with the defenders. Eventually the German attack faded, and as the firing died down the enemy started to pull out backwards – the signallers and cooks, the mule men and the gunners' mates had triumphed. I don't think anyone exactly commanded – it was more a "défense qui peut". But none the less it was decisive.

Our men of course were digging in rapidly on Kef el Tior, but the pickets on the rim soon became aware of muffled noises in the cud sides below them. Peter Sillem and some of 18 Platoon were lying-up there and after a while Peter called me over. I arrived at about the same time as the first detachment of the opposition appeared, returning from their adventures on Bettiour.

They did not appear to be in very good order, perhaps due to their exertions in climbing the cliff as well as having just lost a battle, and they did not know we were there. Their leader, very properly, was well in front of the rest of his straggling troops, and I called across to him "Wollen sie sich ergeben?" or some such, hoping that he would understand my stock phrase request to surrender. However the German snapped round in a flash, and Clanachan and I both sensed unfriendly thoughts in the same split second. We shot together and the man went down in a wailing heap. The remainder of his team quickly put up their hands without futher ado.

There was no time for the usual courtesies, other than to attend to the wounded man. Peter's men quickly disarmed and searched their late foes, then Fincham rounded them up, thirteen of them, and took them back to the battalion H.Q. with the six others taken en route, and some of our own casualties. Dick Jefferies would deal with their onward transmission.

In the meantime there were noises of other parties ascending the cliff side unaware of the reception committee waiting for them at the top. But this matter could be left in Peter's competent hands.

The next posse was very much larger, perhaps the remains of a company. Before they had all reached our rim Peter knew that there were too many to digest. He barged into a German officer who I think mistook him for one of his own men, and an altercation followed. Peter shot the officer, who fell down the cliff, and our picket opened fire on the rest. The Germans ran for it in several directions and vanished in the murk. This kind of thing went on throughout the remainder of the night, some of the opposition coming through us from behind, along the route of our attack.

Before the night was out we had sent back sixty prisoners.

We had won back Djebel Ang and more besides, but whether or not we could hold it was another matter. The new day dawning would soon tell us, but in the meantime its first light glow was lost in those mists, and when the sun at last rose over them that sky would be blood red.

In the long carry back through the hills that night, the men carrying Nicolas Jefferies and our other casualties had lost themselves in the mist. Nick raised himself on the stretcher and looked at the stars, and then at his compass, and brought them home to safety.

He died a few hours later.

11

To Have and To Hold

AFTER THE NIGHT of 15 April, though we did not then know it, the enemy reported that they had been driven from their key positions. That being the case they were more conscious of defeat than we were of victory, and all that we knew in the chaotic end of the night's activities was that we had lunged through our adversary's guard and would now have to parry his counter measures.

The Irish Brigade's objectives had by no means been reached, nor could have been that night with any prospect of holding them afterwards. The key ones, the unapproachable Point 622 and its flanking features, were beyond our power anyway – at that stage.

The Inniskillings had suffered the worst possible luck in their attack on Djebel Tangoucha, which was rearing its ugly head there just beside us. Going in with their usual zest they had half of the Djebel in their hands by midnight, but there had been considerable trouble during the approach march, and for some reason the mules had gone fey. The mules however knew something. As they lumbered along in the wake of the Skins' attack they ran into the German contingent who were just forming up for their disastrous assault upon Djebel Bettiour. The enemy fired in to them immediately, and in the melée that followed they succeeded in shooting, or bolting, most of them. No doubt the collision played its part in wrecking the enemy attack on Bettiour, but it made it impossible for the Skins to stay on Tangoucha when all their tools and other impedimenta for consolidating had vanished over the cud side with the animals which carried them. Our Inniskilling brothers were accordingly hauled back, forty men fewer than when they had started.

On our part we finished the night isolated on our little perch, though we did not then realise it, with a resolute enemy in front and around us on both sides.

Resolute they were too, and this German regiment which fought us on Djebel Ang, and resisted to the final and bitter ending, was quite different to any we had met previously.

The enemy troops here were the Reich's penal battalions. The regiment itself, the 962 Schützen Regiment of the 999th Leichte Division, was composed wholly of undesirables – political suspects, black marketeers and other pet aversions of Himmler, and they were here to be purified. Most of the division's members had been serving long prison sentences and when offered the choice had chosen front line infantry duty as an alternative – shades of the Iron Duke's imperishable army!

These men fought us despite all logic, and they fought like furies, probably in fear of their commanders. They had a carefully selected team of thugs as N.C.Os. in charge of them, all hand picked for the purpose and all quite ready to shoot their luckless soldiers at the slightest excuse. They were also serving under picked officers, and the team's performance vividly illustrates Napoleon's dictum "There are *no* bad soldiers, only . . .", not that I fully agree with the Emperor.

The overall command of this outfit was equally interesting. While the division was on route for Tunisia in March its commander had the ill luck to be shot down into the Mediterranean and, as their own divisional staff was missing, its units apparently operated for the most part directly under the Africa Corps Headquarters. In consequence that message with the loss of Djebel Ang seemingly went straight to the top, to no less than General der Panzertruppe Hans Cramer himself. In the afterlight we could appreciate such a distinguished adversary having, as it were, this personal interest in us.

There was also unavoidable command trouble on our own side, though Nelson's misfortune was hardly comparable to his lamented opponent's watery ending. None the less there was a partial loss of direction in the crisis of the battle, but none of us ever appreciated the reason for it at the time. All we knew was that the grip had somehow slackened, and although Beauchamp of course said not a thing, from the onset at Ang, and for some days afterwards, I think he had largely to fend for himself – and I don't think he knew the reason.

Nelson had in fact been considerably damaged in the aftermath of Djebel el Mahdi. Flattened and half stunned by a mortar bomb that killed his signals officer beside him, he was more battered than he ever admitted, and it is hardly surprising that for some critical days the control of the battle had wobbled. But that was no fault of Nelson's. He was not the kind to give up and he would not have expected anyone else to have done so either.

Beauchamp made the best dispositions that he could during those last hours of the night. His own tactical headquarters with Dick and the signallers was just behind us under the razor-back crest of Kef el Tior, in as horribly exposed a position as it was possible to contemplate, and even Dick thought his C.O. was pushing his luck to extremis. Though Beauchamp in fact could at least see everyone from where he was, and that was what mattered just then.

Beauchamp moved Desmond Gethin up with C Company astride the Kef ridge in support, and then he briefed Mike McDonald, who was just off to command A Company. Mac had an invidious assignment, and he had not even seen the ground through glasses as we all had. A Company had a nasty position to hold round the end of that spur. Lying on our left they were on higher ground than ourselves, with vast rocks and scree everywhere, and far more exposed. I liked it not, and I liked it less as the new day dawned. That low-lying mist was a cloak to D Company and it hid the enemy too. But it did not hide A Company on that spur, for the ridge stood above the fog like a ship riding over the sea. Nor for that matter did it hide Desmond Gethin either, but Dizzy and his careful warriors were usually good at making themselves inconspicuous, and took suitable evasive action with alternative positions on either side of the crest.

As the light improved I wormed my way forward to study the scene. Peering through the crevices of the rim in front of me I could see the projecting ridge of Point 622 – if ridge it could be called. It looked more like a huge edition of Hadrian's Wall with the top broken up. If that was the next objective we should be needing scaling ladders like our men at Badajoz. The enemy were quite invisible, but that meant nothing.

I thought that a closer look might help, and crawled over and into the edge of those rocks. There I encountered my opposite number, and I sat and watched his approach as he picked his way over the rocks, bent on finding the facts as I was. He looked immaculate in his long dark greatcoat, and I thought he was coming right up as I sat there, pistol cocked. But then he saw me and more besides. He paused with his field glasses on us, then ducked and turned – and fled.

The German hauptmann had hardly vanished before the front erupted around us, so maybe he was just having a final look. The devils must have wormed their way up through the mist to A Company and they began their attack by trying to rush them. Within minutes they were well inside and over some of Mac's forward posts – and then 132 Field Regiment was in the line of battle and engulfed in it. The first that James Browne knew of the onslaught was the series of explosions as German grenades were showered in to his command post. He and all save one of his men were hit immediately, but miraculously his radio remained serviceable.

The issue here was fought out in the mist at point blank range, the nearest posts of A Company firing back. James of course put down his defensive artillery fire curtain round the front, but as the enemy were inside this barrier already our guns for once were not effective. Also there had not been time to register them accurately, and 132 Field Regiment for a time could do no more than shoot from their maps.

From D Company's position a hundred or so yards beyond and lower, and invisible from the enemy, we lined our Brens on to the tops that A was holding. If anything had given, the enemy would have got no further, and that was all we could say just then for we were under heavy fire ourselves.

Then the mist lifted and our Vickers detachments opened fire. But what or why they were engaging I was never to know. They continued firing for several minutes, thereby making certain that our vigilant enemy would spot them. Then came the reaction in the vicious spitting blast of one Spandau after another from the long ridge of Point 622, and when they had finished their work our own guns were silent and our men lying dead beside them.

James however was still there and, his first assailants frustrated, he was hitting back against our well hidden adversaries. James himself and one of his signallers were still on their feet, but only his sergeant remained uninjured. While both men did their best with the radio a further shower of grenades burst in and around them. Then hearing German orders being shouted below him, Sergeant Guthrie picked up his tommy gun and vaulted over the edge of the post into an abteilung of German infantry just about to storm into it. Firing into his surprised assailants he killed the officer, and the others bolted back over the scree, leaving their dead commander draped across James's parapet.

Beset thus, James realised his command post was untenable and that fire support from it was impossible. He therefore explained matters to his regiment and gave them the target of his own O.P. Two of his men were dead, and he now told Guthrie to run for it. Regrettably the fifth member of James's team had already done so.

Shortly afterwards he baled out himself.

James made straight down towards the dead ground beside us. Unfortunately he had fifty yards to cover before he got there. The German machine gunners on 622 opened up and their bursts became one continuous roar, the ground ripping up first behind him, then streaking up in fountains at his feet. Then they hit him. He stumbled a little, then was over the crest. But they had hit him repeatedly before he reached safety.

We were now virtually beyond means of communicating, and there seems to have been radio trouble. I had Tommy Wood with me at that stage, doing his best with his mortars, and I knew that we had to get a description of our affairs back to Beauchamp. I asked Tommy to do this, though I cannot imagine my feelings when I did it after both of us had seen what had happened to James. Tommy just said, "Lumme, will I make it?" and then ran like a hare. And he did make it, though the Spandaus followed him across the flat the instant he broke cover, the earth flying at his heels.

The firing never stopped all day, and we spent the whole of it with our opponents in and around us. However I knew by now that the enemy were not going to shift us, and if we held on until nightfall our battle would be won for keeps. It was the longest day that I ever knew, waiting for the dusk to hide us. As the welcome night descended I sent Peter forward with 18 Platoon to seize the rocky ruin on our right front, the start of the 622 ridge. We followed this up with a raid by Sergeant Fred White with part of 16 Platoon. Fred took his men over the rim of our front and across the ground below it, with a view to disinfesting our immediate frontage. This he did with his usual thoroughness. Colliding with the enemy in the dark, Fred and his men shot first, dropped several of them and returned with four prisoners and a number of machine guns. Desmond had acted similarly and added a German mortar detachment, the weapon and crew complete, as his last contribution against the Third Reich. There Dizzy's luck ended, or held, according to how you look at it, for his guardian angels were still vigilant and he survived, somehow, a direct hit on his headquarters from a mountain gun or mortar, engaging over open sights. Perhaps those angels were not yet ready for him.

The long day ended. We had lost nine of our men, but we had hit back at our enemy and were in the ascendant. Ang and Kef el Tior were ours, held against all comers – but this still was only partial victory and dearly bought at that. A Company had suffered heavily, and C on the western flank hardly less so. D Company alone remained in reasonable fighting strength, and for that matter if for no other, the rest of the regiment would depend upon us until our adversaries were finally broken.

12

Kef el Tior

By nightfall on that Friday evening of 16 April 1943 the enemy grip had slackened noticeably, but whether this was the ebb setting in or the prelude to intensified counter measures no one could tell us, and we could only guess the answer for ourselves. There was also the further point that none of us knew for sure what the Germans would like when finally brought to bay.

It should have been apparent by now from the number of prisoners, that 962 Regiment had lost a substantial part of its fighting strength, but there were two other high quality regiments still intact in the immediate vicinity ; 755 of our old friend Oberst Weber's 334th Division, and 756 Regiment, which still had to be put to the test on that dark and ominous foothill known as Longstop, poking out of the murk nearly two thousand feet beneath us. In the meantime both these regiments provided ample means for reinforcing the battered penal battalions and eliminating their assailants on those nasty crests above them.

During this critical phase I think that the handling of intelligence matters was open to serious criticism. Little information ever reached D Company as to the forces we were contending with, and usually all we ever knew of our immediate enemy was what we found out for ourselves. This was especially relevant on Kef el Tior, when all we were sure of was the certainty of being fired at whenever we showed ourselves. We did not know whether we were fighting a company or a whole regiment, and we could not know how brittle that front had now become with food, ammunition, and above all fuel, rapidly failing. But our staffs knew all of these things.

The subject of "communication" is always a difficult one, but I think it was virtually ignored in the First Army, and I know that it was a weak point in our own brigade. The up to date enemy order of battle, and the fighting capacity of every part of it, was of course available daily to our divisional staffs from examination of prisoners, but this essential information did not reach the troops.

This subject was much better handled in later campaigns, perhaps due to the lessons learned in Africa and discovering how much they mattered.

During the daylight fighting on the 16th we had brought the enemy to a stop but we had not repelled him, much less broken him up as had happened so miraculously at the end of the night attack. The battle for Ang and the Kefs was more decisive than ever we knew, due to the shattering of that attack on Bettiour, and the destruction, capture or dispersion of the force that took part in it – and we had won those hills at the end of it. Moreover, we had won the battle of the mind, for the enemy had given up when that day reached its close. There would be no going back now, though we did not then know it.

But we thought our adversaries could do little more, without reinforcement, though it would be unwise to count on it, or to underrate their powers of recuperation. On our part it was absolutely necessary to smite them again before any recovery was possible.

The Faughs would have gone on and seen the thing through, knowing perfectly well that they would have to do it anyway, but there was inexplicable delay while a new brigade plan was put together. Our failure to hit the enemy again on the rebound, while he was still off-balance and reeling, was unfortunate, and one of the factors here may have been the creeping exhaustion among our staff, and Nelson's injuries. We ought to have gone in again that very night.

There were other tactical factors to consider. The Faughs had suffered over a hundred casualties during the battle, and in the daylight fighting on the 16th the German losses were certainly less than ours as they were fighting from prepared positions, perfectly concealed and impervious to our shell fire. The artillery in fact was completely ineffective, and this was hardly surprising when the O.P. party were defending themselves with their pistols during the critical period, instead of directing their guns. Even so, concentrations were of no use to us here, and only exceptional accuracy would prevail. Furthermore our adversaries were so close in that the slightest error in ranging would bring our own shells on top of us.

In the week-long pause that followed, both sides settled down to make life as unpleasant for each other as they could, and we thought wistfully of brother Koch. He had never behaved like this. Our soldiers often referred to him and were inclined to judge all other opponents by the standards of his paratroopers.

Shelling, mortaring and sniping were incessant, and in daylight no movement was possible. We just stayed put in our slit trenches, in relative safety providing we did nothing stupid. In spite of the noise, and a blazing sun that seemed to get progressively hotter, those long days offered rare opportunities for calm reflection. There was little else that one could do save think, and even departing to the nearest shell hole for purposes of nature was a tense business. It was a period of reaction for most of us.

In spite of our circumstances, morale in the company was high, and they were proud of what they had done; though the more thoughtful of them, seeing what lay ahead and what still remained to be captured, wondered if they would ever get out of this place. They knew they could never go back, but most of them just shut their minds to this theme. "Sufficient unto the day" is a good philosophy for a soldier. Most of us, I think, were affected by the drama of the situation, the isolation of our position in the midst of the enemy, and all knew how much depended on us. Also there was the undeniable beauty of our surroundings.

The evening lights from our position on Kef el Tior formed a fantastic backdrop to our weird and unearthly landscape. As the sun set over Djebel Ang to the west behind us, the usual orange glow silhouetting those peaks and dragon's teeth faded imperceptibly through all the colours of the spectrum before the black night descended. Then the hills themselves lost their grim outlines, beginning with our own Highland pinks and, at the last, turning into misty white as the stars came out.

I chose this time to write breaking matters off with the charming lass who had lately attracted me. Mother was much interested in this news from my slit trench on Kef el Tior. Replying she observed soothingly, "A dog is much less trouble and gives one a much better return". What father must have thought, had he sighted that passage before the letter's despatch, I cannot think. He had been married to my mother for thirty years.

17 Platoon were on the extreme right of our position beside the southern escarpment, and they were bothered by their inability to picket the edge of it until nightfall. Even then it was hazardous. Immediately below was the village of Heidous, still packed with Hun soldiery, and still resolute for Hitler. They were also beyond our reach, and a particularly bloody-minded lot too. On the top of our cliff just a thousand feet higher, all movement on our part was silhouetted. They had not got a hope of coming up, nor had we any desire to descend, and although never the twain should meet at least we could shoot.

Unfortunately they could shoot better and, when we moved some of our men over to the cliff edge in the moonlight, the denizens below with their telescopic sights set about them. However careful we were, we were skylined on the cliff top, whereas Himmler's untouchables down at the bottom had an infinite variety of cover and could shoot through the roofs of the Berber croftings and woggeries with impunity.

The situation was becoming intolerable, and we put in our pious marksman Fusilier Henry to see what he could do. Holy Henry usually referred to the Scriptures before disturbing the peace, but on this occasion he was not in favour and the enemy outshot him. They hit Henry almost immediately, though not dangerously, and then they as near as a toucher got Robbie, missing him by an inch or so. They also hit Johnston, Henry's mate, and finally they shot Alec Smith through the leg, Alec then being in charge of the sector. Those snipers had earned their keep for the Fatherland.

I talked to Beauchamp and our gunners about the nuisance, and 132 Field Regiment thought that one of the heavy batteries would both cure it and be the better for accurate target practice. The following morning the 7.2s. set to work firing slowly and methodically, though stirring all D Company to extreme apprehension as the flight line of their shells was exactly parallel to our southern front. Furthermore although we were over a thousand feet from the target in the vertical plane, horizontally we were scarcely a pistol shot from it. These colossal shells came past us like the screaming whistle of a Stuka. Most of the army's gun barrels were pretty badly worn by now, and we did not care for these over-fine limits, but in fact that day the fuses were being temperamental and over half of our shells were duds, pitching into Heidous with a shuddering thump that achieved nothing save bringing down showers of scree from the cliff face. The remainder went off with the blast of an aircraft bomb, with dense palls of smoke rising high above us and blotting out all sight of the village beneath.

I must say they did stop the sniping, though in later times gunners were apt to comment at cocktail parties about our expensive methods of quelling enemy riflemen.

After the light had gone and with these horrible noises still going on below us from the 7.2s., Peter took a small raiding party down the 622 ridge to forestall any devilment during the night.

As he and his men crawled silently over the rocks in the starlight he came across a small posse of Germans doing likewise. While he sat there and waited for them, the enemy jugged down and started to mount one of their Spandaus twenty or so yards in front of him, tripod and all. An ignorant and careless crew, they made so much noise that they failed to notice Peter's silent surrounding of them, and he picked up the lot – three of them, and their gun, without a shot, a sound or a word said. It is usually disconcerting when one's men disappear during the night, as we well knew ourselves, and I hope that our hauptmann friend opposite slept less easily afterwards, that is if he slept at all when commanding such an outfit.

Peter had done well.

The London Irish Rifles were now back in the fold, to everyone's relief, after their month-long convalescence, and at this stage they could be said to be the only fresh and intact battalion in the 78th Division. However with a virtually new team they had little time to get to know each other and care was necessary to begin with. It was a comforting feeling that Pat Scott was beside us once more, down in those dips beyond Bettiour. And even more so as he began to probe gently in and around Heidous.

During the afternoon of the 18th he sent James Dunnill with F Company of the Rifles to see if he could get in to the place, but I do not think that any of us appreciated just then the function of that wretched village in the enemy defence system. It was really only an outwork of the main hill defences behind it, and as the Germans had seen fit to hold it quite strongly it was perhaps best ignored. Certainly it was not a place to take on in isolation. Weber's 755 Regiment were down there somewhere, though I think that the Germans had been thinning out their front, and were holding the sector below us principally by fire.

James had very wisely been specifically warned against getting committed, and he was given a free hand to act as he thought fit, the only proviso being to avoid at all costs the risk of repulse. This operation was a try-on, and had it been otherwise half the brigade could have found itself involved. None the less James managed to cause a considerable stir.

After last night's bombardment, and now with further concentrations coming down on the village, the enemy I think assumed that a major attack was in progress and put down full scale defensive fire on us as well as around his old positions in front of Heidous. In consequence we lost two more of our men, and James was not able to do much to annoy the village. Heidous was then a problem and in the end would be squeezed out. It never fell to assault.

The Germans were unpleasantly accurate in their shelling. Using some of their own mediums they half buried several of our warriors in their slit trenches and we had to dig them out at the conclusion. Among them was Peter's platoon sergeant, Murphy, who was so battered that we had to evacuate him. Bartram accordingly put up his third stripe in his place.

The last casualty that evening was Lance Corporal James Given, who now took his leave of this world in a manner that was quite exceptional even in Faugh history, though entirely in keeping with Given's form. The corporal, to give him his final title on this earth, was hit in the last bombardment that evening. He was actually sharing a weapon pit with Sid Smith 05 at the time, but

Sid found his field dressing inadequate to cope with the splinter slash across his section commander's forehead. So James Given was brought over to my H.Q., and we sent him back to the R.A.P. for the M.O.'s attention. We should have warned Bill that our little treasure was on his way. Having done what was necessary with Given, the good doctor was dealing with other matters while Given took his opportunity. He found the medical rum supplies, acted predictably, and in a few minutes was fighting drunk. Reeling out of the M.I. tent he headed back to the battle and the Inniskillings found him a week later, lying dead in the German positions on the col of Tangoucha after we had finally captured the place.

James Given was a good disciplinarian in the line, and any fusilier who argued with him was liable to be brained with a rifle butt. He was a true Faugh, with simple tastes – rum and the regiment.

Later that night I went back to the Tac H.Q. for a few minutes, to chat with Dick and condole over his brother. There was always rum as our panacea for all troubles, and anyway he was running a battle which, to use his own words, did not stop because of Nicolas. The Almighty seemed to armour one against the wrong sort of reflections, and everything could be pushed into the background in a kind of dull though remote detachment. The aches could come later, but in the meantime when death was a daily visitor there was no course open save to battle on, knowing that all was pre-ordained anyway.

The following evening Beauchamp came in to see us at dusk, actually bringing the rum ration with him and personally escorted by Colour Sergeant David Bartlett. He spent most of the evening with us, first chatting over our rum and then crawling along our rim, studying the deep draw beyond and the battlements of the Point 622 ridge opposite. Dusk was a good time to do this, with the afterglow in the west behind us, for one was virtually invisible to the enemy while it persisted. After this prowl was over, Beauchamp knew pretty well where the enemy were sited; at least he knew what I knew, though this was by no means conclusive.

Beauchamp himself was a considerable source of concern both to Dick Jefferies and to me, due to his alarming habit of visiting the front line at strange hours, often without warning or escort.

Writing about it recently Dick said that being adjutant to Beauchamp was a pretty hair-raising business, and he had to have a system of spies to see that his C.O. didn't disappear into the night without some kind of bodyguard. Dave Bartlett's arrival with his colonel that evening was by no means coincidental.

Six months later, alas, Beauchamp met his death acting exactly as he had done during that night on Ang, pushing forward alone in the darkness when his forward companies were in trouble.

Later that night on Kef el Tior he gave me the outline plan of the battle intended for two nights hence. He could indicate little to us then save the date and that we were being cast in the lead part again. All this was very flattering, though modified by knowing that there was no other course open to Beauchamp, and if we could not capture that damnable redoubt in front of us I did not know who could. There was no one else.

The next day, 20 April, for some unknown reason was one of tension. Other than it being the Führer's birthday there was no particular reason for it as it had been quieter than usual for most of the time. Admittedly it was exceedingly hot, and we became very conscious of the intensity of the African glare as the sun beat down upon us in our weapon pits. In the middle of the day one of our fusiliers suddenly jumped out of his trench and went berserk. He ran completely amok, and started screaming and waving his rifle like a follower of the Prophet about to slaughter an infidel. Scratching up my knowledge of Wren's Foreign Legion stories I think that the French would have called it Le Cafard – a term which I understand is accepted in the French colonial army as an excuse for virtually any kind of misconduct.

The C.S.M. got up and walked over towards me, evidently with the thought of explaining; however he thought better of it, apparently deciding to spare me any vexatious decision. Instead he turned on his heel and walked slowly over to the man, eyed him for a moment, and then smashed him to the ground with a blow that would have flattened a bullock. Then he dragged the man over and dumped him in the nearest slit trench like a bag of rotting potatoes.

Fred then walked back to me and could think of nothing better to say than that the day was getting a trifle warm, or words to that effect.

Disciplinary problems were easily solved in the line, and anyway why bother the C.O. with vexatious trivia. Whatever we did Beauchamp and Dick would sort the thing out when once the campaign was over, in the unlikely event of it ever being necessary.

The day following, 21 April, we spent getting ready for battle, as far as the circumstances allowed it.

Fincham came in during the afternoon and told me that my despatch rider, Fusilier Porter, had been killed by mortar fire when coming up with the mules. Porter was an old and trusted friend and had been with us for years. I still have the sweet letters of his wife "and baby daughter Elizabeth".

Later that evening the C.S.M. dropped in to my slit trench as usual, and we consumed our rum together. We chatted for quite a long time as we often did, and Fred referred to Porter, who was on both our minds. Then he remarked, "You know, sir, up to now I have never thought much about my chances of surviving. I have always thought that I would make it somehow and I have never bothered about it." He took the matter a little further and made some lighthearted remarks about the battle in front of us. Finally he said, "And now I am not so sure, but I can't say it worries me" or words to that effect. I made some commonplace comments about not thinking about it either, and that there was always too much to do, looking after our pack of lunatics in D Company.

We spent most of that evening drinking rum together, and picking at some of the canned fruit out of the compo packs, all that any of us ever ate during those days on Kef el Tior.

I think that we shut our minds to the problem confronting us the following night, and brushed it aside at the time as a rather nasty thought. Afterwards, brooding over the matter in hospital I thought that we had been absolutely mad, and myself the maddest. I am sorry to say that our task had nothing like the consideration that it merited, either by me or by anyone else who was involved in it. Mentally I suppose we were in a rather sluggish state, and the constant shelling and mortar fire of the last week may have partly induced this negligent attitude. I think that temporarily we had lost our capacity for careful attention to detail which alone could have ensured success.

None the less, whether we recognised it or not, our worst battle so far lay in front of us, and it was also the worst laid-on one. This was not one of our brightest moments. Another factor was the fighting strength of the company. With thirty-five battle casualties since the onset at Mahdi a fortnight back, we were now down to fifty, and with the loss of so many N.C.Os., including veterans like Murphy and Corporal Flowers, the normal organisation for fighting was no longer possible. Peter alone remained of the company officers apart from myself, and we had five N.C.Os. left other than Fred Fincham and the colour sergeant.

We had better win our battle quickly before worse befell.

13

St. George's Day 1943

OUR OBJECTIVE THAT night merits some description, for as a defensive position it was unique, even by German standards. The Point 622 ridge ran out from our right front in a kind of curl. I described it as looking like a mammoth Hadrian's Wall. In fact it was more like a harbour mole jutting out over a steeply shelving beach.

The thing was cliff-sided, about ten feet high our end, which we held, deepening to perhaps fifty feet at the other end of the feature. Nature had gone mad with its top – about twenty yards wide, it was broken up like a blown-up rampart.

A little over three hundred yards from us Point 622 itself projected above all this natural litter – another solid slab of rock sticking up like a sawn-off martello tower, with rubble around it from apex to base.

The Point was literally the key point of this, their Siegfried Line as the enemy called it. They had been there for months, perfecting it with their usual ingenuity in defensive works.

Their engineers had burrowed in to this vast natural chunk of concrete and had produced underground quarters for themselves like miniature Aladdin's caves, and these residences were virtually impervious to shell fire.

All they had to do when disturbed was to sit in the top of their fortress with grenades by the sackful and toss them over the side at suitable intervals. They could defend it without even interrupting their dinner.

There were however fissures which here and there ran up the side of the thing – which it was possible to scale, one man at a time, assisting each other.

On the right of the 622 ridge – though it hardly merited so polite a geographical term – grew the roots of Djebel Tangoucha, spreading southwards and upwards, with a relatively smooth col joining the two features just beyond Point 622 itself. That col was level with the top of the ridge so that both features were mutually supporting.

Way over left was another lump of a feature; named after Beauchamp and thereafter immortalised in regimental history as Butler's Hill, this position was just outside D Company's sector.

The Germans did the obvious thing by holding 622 and Butler's Hill in strength, with a line of pickets at night between them. They also held the whole length of the Tangoucha col.

Djebel Tangoucha itself was not held, save from its flanks, like the notorious Longstop Hill below it. Point 622, and the col between them, covered all of the Djebel – the front, the reverse and the top. It is not surprising that the Inniskillings found their task at Tangoucha an impossible one, and when 622 was eventually taken the Skins walked straight over the feature without further opposition. The battle for Tangoucha was a battle for its approaches and flanks, and the same applied to its evil neighbour beneath it.

Months later Nelson looked at our battlefield with the corps commander. Referring to our men, he recorded that his companion had asked, "How on earth did they do it?" Nelson said that he could reply quite truthfully, "I'm damned if I know."

In the afterlight, and much thought about it, I think we might have tried the Chinese water torture trick. That is if an accurate enough gun could have been found to do it. This interesting technique was used occasionally in Italy later, and required registering a single gun exactly on to the target, firing one shell at precise time intervals – say five minutes – and continuing the treatment indefinitely. It might have driven the occupants mad after a while, particularly if a 7.2 had been available for the task.

One other thing we most certainly ought to have done was to drown the whole area in smoke, and kept it like that throughout the night of our attack. With our small force there was no need for anyone to lose themselves, and no one could have had the least doubt as to their whereabouts. They were either on that ridge or they had fallen over the edge of it and would no longer be interested. But one thing the enemy defence *did* depend on was vision.

The plan of operations for the night shows how far we were below our usual form. In the battalion we knew perfectly well where at least some of the enemy were, but this information had not been absorbed at a higher level – or, if it had, it was not acted on. On our part we underestimated both the German strength and fighting capacity, an error of thought which was probably magnified by giving our adversaries a week to recover themselves and to reinforce the sector.

Beauchamp gave his orders at dusk and we discussed them for a while, both of us knowing perfectly well that they did not exactly fit the circumstances. D Company's task that night was simply to capture the Point 622 ridge. The Inniskillings were going to have another go at Tangoucha again, for the third time, and the available artillery would all be put down first on Heidous and then on the Djebel, where of course there were no enemy in the physical sense, though we could be sure of a deluge of mortar fire and all else on it. Tangoucha was held by fire and not men, and we both knew this. The London Irish were attacking Heidous again at the same time as the Inniskillings went in.

Butler's Hill, the other half of the German defensive zone, was not provided for. It was neither attacked that night, presumably because there was no one left to attack it, nor was it included in the fire plan as a target essential to neutralise.

So far as the Faughs were concerned this was simply a night attack by one company without fire support, and it may well have been the best thing to do. At least it was a limited stake.

Our men were not particularly bothered. They had succeeded in everything so far, so why should they be. My briefing of them was more like that for a fighting patrol than for fighting a battle, and far too much was left to chance.

I simply asked Peter to get up out of his position at 9.30 p.m. when the bombardment of Tangoucha began, and push as fast and as far as he could get with 18 Platoon – now about fifteen strong – and get on to the 622 hump somehow if he could. I was going to take the rest of the company across the falling ground between 622 and Butler's Hill, clear the area of the enemy and then join Peter on the ridge. After this the rest of the ridge, not in Peter's hands, and the Tangoucha col, could have our undivided attention.

There was very heavy shelling at dusk after Beauchamp had finished his orders – almost defensive fire intensity, beginning with the German field artillery, then joining up with the 5.9s., the whole thickened up with mortars. The top of the Kef el Tior feature erupted and the German shells were screaming down in wild pandemonium all over it. They could be attacking us and I wondered – were they? If so we could repeat our parry and riposte of 15 April to even greater advantage. That is if we could ever get out of our positions to form our line of battle. This was a tense enough business at any time, but it was almost a desperate one at 9 p.m. on the evening of 22 April with that firestorm coming down upon us.

However we got going somehow, and we made flat out in ones and twos over to 18 Platoon's position in the saddle on the end of the ridge. This was on the fringe of the concentrations coming down on Kef el Tior, and being hard up to the enemy forward defences we were almost inside their fire curtain. I was heartily relieved when we were all safely in that saddle with our men lying down quietly, Peter and his men on the right, waiting for our little zero hour, and I didn't think many gentlemen of England now abed would think themselves accursed that they weren't with us, not that I think our men needed Shakespeare to inspire them.

As for this extraordinarily heavy bombardment, the Germans were either anticipating or acting on intuition.

At 9.30 p.m. we hitched up our rifles, slung our Brens in to the hip position, and set off into the night, Beauchamp bringing his Tac H.Q. forward in to our positions as we moved off.

Then our artillery came down on Tangoucha and Heidous. At least this was a distraction for our opponents, even if nothing else was achieved.

The opposition was heavy and immediate and afterwards I wondered what exactly the Germans themselves had been contemplating that evening.

Peter with 18 Platoon picked his way along the top of the ridge, but he did not get very far before the enemy opened up on him with small arms – rifles and schmeissers. As we were immediately below 18 Platoon we could see them creeping forward outlined against the sky, and once or twice heaving grenades at the unseen enemy pickets. This was very encouraging, and after the flash and roar of the explosions just over our heads I hoped that Peter would remember we were only twenty feet below him.

We only had moments to consider Peter's problems. Moving down the draw in line we encountered a number of the opposition coming up the draw towards us – faint shadows coming out of the ground in the darkness. We fired into them immediately with our Brens, and the criss-crossing streams of tracer had their usual effect. The enemy line melted. There were not a lot of them and we picked up half a dozen who obligingly surrendered. The rest vanished. We disarmed the prisoners and sent them back to the C.O. with two of our men, and continued. Beauchamp should have had quite a good view up there on the top of the rim two hundred yards back.

This incident and ensuing commotion was quite enough for us to lose touch with Peter, and moreover the noise of the shooting stirred up the Butler's Hill hornets' nest. A stream of parachute flares and Very lights soared up into the sky and turned the draw into a fairground – the only saving grace being the black shadows cast by the rocks which became ever blacker and denser by contrast under the vivid intensity of the German flares. The German pickets had carried out their function, if not very bravely.

The next thing we knew was a hideous explosion against the cliff face opposite as the Butler's Hill garrison let rip with one of their mountain guns or some equally foul contrivance ; they followed this up seconds later with their Spandaus, whose screeching banshee howl came right through us and dissolved against the rocks at our feet into a shower of sparks and ricocheting tracer. Fortunately they could only see us momentarily in those shadows, and diving for cover we were able to crawl beyond their vision. But the one burst brought down all my Tac H.Q., signallers, orderly, and my faithful Clanachan.

After this we were relatively safe as we moved down the draw, leaving the Germans industriously firing into the scene of the last encounter and well behind us. However if we were safe, Jack Birch and his mates, our stretcher bearers, were by no means so as they did their best for our men under that hail of bullets. Mercifully the enemy were firing slightly high.

We had crawled on perhaps another hundred yards or so and then got to our feet again. Almost immediately the German posts below 622 opened up from ahead of us. Spread out like that we were not much of a target, and again the enemy were high. Our men fired back instantly from the hip, and with the tendency always to shoot low from this position our tracer went streaking into the ground in front of the opposition, ricocheting into and through them and accompanied by showers of fragmented rock. They stood it for perhaps a minute, just long enough for our Bren gunners to whip on their second magazines, and then they upped and bolted to a man.

This was almost the end of act one of the programme, and with the low ground disinfested we could rejoin Peter, at least safe on our northern flank. So we swung round in a circle and immediately picked up another two or three Germans who had probably been watching Beauchamp up near the rim. We had come up behind them and they were just sitting there – skylined to us. They made no fuss and dropped their weapons as soon as they saw us, scarcely ten yards from them.

At this stage the Germans could hardly know our whereabouts or our strength. They knew that they had Peter in front of them on the ridge, but we were in the shadows of the draw and well below the line of sight of either garrison, 622 or Butler's Hill.

We found Peter again by the expedient of working back half way to our starting point, climbing on to the ridge, and then following along until we came up with his men. Peter in fact was doing quite well as his platoon crawled through the rocks, and one by one they were shooting out the opposition.

This sniping match going on in the dark was not a very accurate affair, but the opposition were none the less pulling out and crawling back to other posts. However there was no bolting or throwing in the towel as had occurred down below.

By the time I had found Peter and crawled up to him he was

about a hundred yards from Point 622 itself, and the rocky citadel was gleaming there just ahead of us, white and stark under the stars, with perhaps twenty yards of relatively smooth plinth-like rock in front of it. There was no cover there.

Heavy rifle fire and an occasional grenade was coming from the Point just then, with sporadic Spandau bursts whipping across from the col which lay just beyond and half right of our target. Tangoucha gleamed fitfully beside us with our own shells still coming down on it in periodic salvoes. The concentrations had long since stopped and the Skins were somewhere over there – below us and not far off.

I sent 16 and 17 Platoons back and down with Fred White and Morrisey to see if they could get on to the ridge behind Point 622, and in fact after a while Fred succeeded in doing this, our warriors scaling up the crevices like the forlorn hope at Cuidad Rodrigo. The enemy showered grenades on to them from the top as they did so, and only the boiling oil was lacking to add colour to a military operation which bore all the imprint of the Middle Ages. Fred and his men achieved their climb almost unscathed at the time as most of the German grenades bounced all the way to the bottom before they exploded, a tactical point not realised by the humourless garrison above them.

Sergeant Morrisey waited until 16 Platoon were safely on top before attempting the climb himself, and this slight delay resulted in chaos so complete that neither side could resolve it.

To begin with Fred managed to clear the ridge in his immediate vicinity, or at least the opposition withdrew into the shadows as soon as his men were up there and shooting. But before 17 Platoon followed suit the hauptmann commanding sent in more of his minions, and when Morrisey and Robbie attempted the climb they found a dozen or so of the enemy lining the top instead of Fred's helping hands.

Confusion absolute now descended, and for a short time neither side could identify the other. The Germans shot indiscriminately in to both, and we were not much better. Corporal Jennings scaled one of the crevices without the rest of his men realising that he had done so, and as he was immediately set upon by several of the enemy at the top, he promptly jumped back. Mallon mistook his corporal for a descending German, and put five bullets through Jennings' legs before realising his error. Smith 05 and Dusty Miller pushed on up the next crevice, and had nearly reached the top when they were also fired into by a number of the enemy, who were leaning over the edge and discharging their automatic rifles straight down the crevice. They missed Sid Smith at a range of less than three yards, and Dusty escaped simply by rolling down to the bottom again. Sid's number three followed him, the butt of his rifle being shot off the weapon as he drew on one of his assailants.

In spite of these trials all of 17 Platoon one way or another did get up on to the ridge in the end, finding here and there fissures which had escaped the notice of our unobservant opponents. Once on top, 17 Platoon shot it out with them and before long most of them had departed. Their dead still lay scattered over that desolate ridge when the battle finally ended two days later.

We now had the ridge of 622 occupied at each end, but not in the middle round 622, nor the col, nor Butler's Hill which was well beyond our reach.

The defenders of Point 622 were resolute enough and we had a first-class view of their methods. The fight went on for over five hours so they clearly had immense stocks of grenades and ammunition. There was a continuous flicker of light from its crest as they shot at us, but a lot of it was very far from being aimed fire. They were tossing grenades out all around the thing, and periodically firing rifle grenades off into the night in any direction that took their fancy. There was one particular gentleman who had one of their not very effective automatic rifles. About once every minute he got to his feet, leaned over the parapet and, as fast as it was possible to fire the thing, he discharged the ten shots from his weapon in to the void below; then he dived back into his hole like a jack in the box to reload. It occurred to me that we could eliminate him without undue difficulty.

Whether or not this team was a bunch of picked men or whether the hauptmann and his iron-fisted N.C.Os. were just behind their men on that ridge I was never to know; I expect that they were, and it would explain the unwillingness to retreat. We knew from our prisoners both the strange make-up of their regiment and the attitude of the soldaten to their superiors, and I suppose fear of one's officers, if absolute enough, was one way to ensure satisfactory conduct in battle.

The German soldiers on the ridge that night had problems. If they withdrew they would be shot by their own side, if they pushed forward they would be shot by us, and if they skipped sideways they would fall over the cliff.

So they had only one option remaining, and fought it out in their posts.

At least the garrison were making an impressive noise on behalf of the Fatherland, but inevitably in that intensity of fire some of their shots went home. 16 and 17 Platoons both had about ten men left on their feet and ought to have been working as one group, but with the enemy on both sides of them they were firing back to back and tending to separate. Then Robbie himself was hit. In the meantime 18 Platoon, with Peter, was still fairly intact, not having been exposed like the rest of the company.

I picked up one of Peter's Brens, borrowed Bartram and one of his fusiliers, and collecting all the magazines within reach the three of us crawled forward into a nice comfortable firing position between a couple of boulders.

Here we had a first class view of Point 622, now about fifty yards off, with its castellated battlements outlined against the starry sky behind them. Setting the gun for single-shot firing I dropped my eye below the line of the barrel and set to work firing at the flashes. When the tracer started to ricochet and streak off up into the sky from the edges of those rocks in front, I knew we were on.

I think that we got the gentleman with the automatic rifle quickly enough, simply by opening fire after the required interval when he was next due to appear. After a while we had used up most of the half dozen or so magazines which Bartram and his assistant had brought with them, and I noticed that the target itself was silent. As we stopped firing the whole battlefield quietened – not only here but on Tangoucha too; hardly a gun was firing now. I got up and walked across to the other side of the ridge. Still relatively quiet. Then there was a vicious crack almost under my feet, and my water bottle whipped up against my forearm, decanting its contents at the same time. Reacting mindlessly I undid the thing and heaved it over the cud in disgust. Then thinking that the rifle shot had come from the col, I withdrew hurriedly and went back to 18 Platoon. Here I found that we had no grenades left and that the few Bren magazines still in our possession were all empty. Bartram I think refilled a few. The rest were scattered about the hillside where they had been used. I am afraid that in night actions our excited men often forgot these necessities.

There was a rather more protracted pause while we considered, and I said to Peter that I thought we might get in to 622 if we kept well out of sight from the col. But there was not much time left to do it.

Bartram and two or three others came with me, well spread out, while Peter and the rest of 18 Platoon covered us.

Walking across those last few yards of bare rock the night suddenly seemed intensely bright. It was also empty and unworldly, but perhaps it was like that in other ages when crossing the glacis. The whole weird landscape seemed devoid of life as I got on to, and up, over the rocks of the Point.

Then my run of luck ended.

There were just a couple of clinks as that damnable stick grenade bounced down to my feet. Then the sky in front of me turned into roaring flame with sledge-hammers mixed into it, and time for a while stood still.

As I sat there, temporarily blinded, the other German posts came to life with a vengeance, the battle erupting again with blasts of schmeisser and rifle fire from the col, and solid streams of tracer whipping into and over the ridge from the machine gunners on Butler's Hill. They began by firing straight in to their own men on the Point, and as Peter's men shot back, Morrisey and Fred, on the other side, took cover from the hail of bullets coming through them impartially from both sides.

After a while Bartram crawled up to me and I asked him to get Mr Sillem. Eventually Peter came and we discussed our situation, knowing that the first faint traces of light were already evident over the eastern hills. There was no time left to us now. I said, "Peter, get in to that thing if you can do it now, but don't wait any longer. Otherwise you have got to get all the men back before daylight. I'm afraid we have made a cock of it." Peter said he would do what he could, and my staunch subaltern made good his promise two days later.

In the meantime he had a trying hour ahead of him, recovering the remains of 16 and 17 Platoons who were inextricably mixed with the enemy and separated from each other on the far side of the Point. By this time some of the team were past caring, and the rounding up was carried out with a reckless abandon. Peter left most of his men on the ridge, and taking two or three with him he climbed down in search of the lost sheep. Calling up from the bottom of the cliff as they hunted along for Fred and his men, the usual reply was a burst from a schmeisser, until at last Fred's cheerful voice came floating down from the battlements above. Fred was in personal trouble too. He was full of splinters and his glasses had been blown in. As he was as blind as a bat without them he could hardly be said to be in full control of the situation.

This part and the rest of the account of the battle comes from Beauchamp himself, and from Fred White, and from our other characters who came through it, and in particular from Denis Hayward who took over – and those heroic scallywags Fusilier Mallon and Corporal Swain, who were usually in trouble out of the line and indispensable in it.

My part in proceedings ended I recall little further, and nothing as to how I got back. There was an anxious Beauchamp seeking of course to save the battle, but that was impossible that night with the dawn now breaking. Then that wretched M.O. "Getting careless, aren't you?" he murmured pleasantly, as he applied some foul concoction to put me out for the next week.

We had lost nineteen of our men, and we had also lost the battle. But it was now St. George's Day and we would win the next one.

14

The Fatal Hill

We now know that our attack had broken down like some of those German ones in earlier days, and for the same reasons. An assault of that kind would only be likely to succeed if carried straight through in one operation, but once the opposing forces were inextricably mixed further momentum was hardly possible without diversion from another quarter.

We could have won had the enemy's resolution suddenly failed them, as might well have happened with other troops. These, however, were above average – at least their officers and N.C.Os. were, and they showed not the slightest signs of giving way. Those whom we captured, drove out, or shot out that night owed their demise either to the shock of surprise or the fact that we were usually more effective, accurate and quicker, with our weapons.

In our case only some miracle with the Inniskilling attack could have helped us, but the Skins could not win their battle until we had won ours first.

There were of course other factors, as there was serious misappreciation in the overall plan of the battle. But it is easy to be wise in the afterlight, and logical thought in later days overlooks the general opaqueness of the scene, and the mental and physical state of the combatants on both sides at that stage of our offensive.

None the less my part in the proceedings bears no examination whatever, as I had concluded my four year command with my company completely out of control, and with a resolute and bloody-minded enemy squarely in the middle of the two halves of it. Under these circumstances, in accordance with the usual rules, our surviving antagonists only had to remain in their posts to win the battle. I had indeed achieved the absolute in terms of military shambles, and my observations to Peter, almost my last words ever to him, were the stark truth.

All this left much to brood upon in the weeks to come, when there was little else to do save brood. Still there were other factors. Our adversaries could have been left in no doubt of our fighting capacity, and in this respect at least there could be no reproach. In my experience there was never another action quite like this, where our men were engaged at point-blank range through the whole course of a night. Not one of them turned their backs, nor ever showed the slightest disposition to do so. Nor was a single man of ours lost that night to the enemy. The ultimate failure was no fault of theirs and the manner of the withdrawal speaks for itself.

Nor was there loss of confidence in spite of the patent lapse of management. They knew we did not make a habit of such things, and they also knew perfectly well that the withdrawal was only tactical, as we could not have stayed alive on that ridge in daylight unless we had eliminated the whole of the local garrison.

As the battle ended there were the remnants of a German company at the end of the ridge sitting around Fred White, though they were just as split up as we were. There was also the intact garrison of the Tangoucha col which we never reached that night, though scarcely a pistol shot beyond 17 Platoon's last positions. Then there were the fortunate occupants of Butler's Hill who, not being called on to defend themselves personally, maintained themselves during the night by firing continuously and impartially in to both sides. We were never to know if we had silenced the Point 622 citadel itself. All firing from it had ceased. That is all we could say, but the residents had probably gone to ground in the cave beneath it.

Peter did not leave until 5 a.m. when it was beginning to get light, and it had taken up all of the intervening time to get the company together again. As he brought back our battered and frustrated warriors he simply reoccupied his old posts which 18 Platoon had held previously on our end of the 622 ridge.

D Company was now thirty-one strong, including the colour

sergeant, the cooks and the mule team. Peter had one survivor of our tactical headquarters, and 18 Platoon had thirteen men including himself. The other two platoons put together were only a handful.

When the dawn broke the battlefield quietened as had sometimes happened before in the aftermath of conflict, and a tacit truce followed. The German stretcher bearers were active, and sensing the attitude, Peter sent Jack Birch and Cooke out, though we had in fact recovered our men before the night had ended. Stretcher parties were rarely molested and never deliberately in my experience. Both sides observed the decencies wherever it was possible to do so – and they did so now, well knowing the helpless plight of men struck down and lost in night encounters. In such an aftermath all succour was impartial, and the rescuer a friend to whoever needed him, regardless of nationality.

That day no one fired, but the mist came down thick in the evening and the following morning was shrouded in fog.

During these two days Nelson found another weapon to add to the discomfiture of our adversaries, and it was probably decisive in finally breaking their determination. But it was only possible to use it through our good fortune in having tank men by us who were not put off by the obstacles around them when most others would have been.

Our cavalry regiment, the North Irish Horse, were free of the inhibitions sometimes found in traditionally-minded units. They did not consider that all hunting should be over flat country, and they did not mind about their machines. Yes, they might get a tank or two up the three thousand feet over Djebel Ang, and if they couldn't get them down again they would no doubt be given others.

So they set off to prove it, with seventy mules behind them loaded with petrol.

Two days later they had done it. Three of them, and they were the only power-driven vehicles ever to get over Ang. It was scarcely mule country, as Nelson observed later, but he had now got three aces tucked up his sleeve for his last hand of poker with brother Hans Cramer opposite.

I do not think that anyone can appreciate the achievement of the

North Irish Horse tank crews unless they had carried out that climb themselves, preferably in charge of a mule column. Nothing in Italy, or elsewhere in my experience, was comparable to those trackless and precipitous mountain wastes, fit only for the Berber goats and shunned even by them. In our own islands I think one would have to go to the Glencoe hills to find their equal.

By nightfall on 24 April these three Churchill tanks were hull down on Kef el Tior awaiting the morning.

In the meantime Peter had been joined by Lieutenant Denis Hayward, who had only come to the battalion two nights previously, and was about to experience as rugged an initiation as ever fell to the lot of a Faugh officer. Fortunately Denis was well equipped to cope with the drama awaiting him. An unemotional and self-confident character he showed little concern for his surroundings and simply got on with the job, making himself at home with our men in spite of their indifferent circumstances. His arrival was a tonic for D Company at a time when one was obviously needed, and he was a pretty good match for Peter himself.

Other moves also had to be made. Fred White was one of the casualties of the night attack, but with superficial damage he was still mobile, though unable to perform competently in battle without his glasses. So Peter did a straight swop with the colour sergeant. Dave Bartlett was fished out of our rear headquarters, where he was in charge of the mules, to take over an amalgam of 16 and 18 Platoons, while Sergeant Morrisey, the only other senior N.C.O. left, commanded the rest.

The following morning Beauchamp organised a further effort by A and D Companies together. Both of them were now about thirty strong. Whether it would have proved to be a last effort nobody can ever say, but I suppose it was getting near the ultimate as another battle like the last one would have left matters like the last hour at Thermopylae. What was perhaps not fully realised was that the Germans themselves had reached their breaking point and knew it, whereas in our case no one had either thought about it or considered the matter. If they had it had certainly never reached Beauchamp's ears – or mine for that matter.

In fact the continual attrition which the enemy had suffered lately was as much to do with the mind as with other factors.

Though considerably weakened, their fighting strength on our front was still as high as ours, or higher, though probably inadequate to hold their scattered outposts over that broken front. But with fundamentals like rations failing, they knew that no hope remained, and when their fragile mountain line was finally pierced it is not surprising that the German defence of Tunisia collapsed like the card castle it was.

When the daylight came the battlefield still remained quiet as the tank crews waited, with dense shimmering Highland mist swirling around them.

In the end Beauchamp's main concern, and that of the North Irish Horse troop commander, was to ensure the maximum visibility for the gun crews, so that they could see down the sights of the tanks' six pounders, and Besa machine guns, into those crags and crevices which provided such perfect concealment to the enemy. Both men waited patiently for the mist to lift. So did the veteran survivors of A and D Company, whose thoughts require no imagination by those who have experienced pre-battle tension and can picture the extremity of their circumstances. Peter and his soldiers waited for four hours behind their weapons during that morning of 25 April 1943.

The afternoon had come when Beauchamp at last gave the signal for the attack, and our sixty-odd Faughs, who alone remained to fight, were committed to battle on issues no less than those that Marlborough fought for with sixty thousand against the regal aggressor of his day.

As the divisional artillery concentrations were put down on Point 622, the three North Irish Horse Churchills crawled on to the crest, and then down the draw spreading out beneath them. At ranges of a hundred yards or so they fired solid shot, high explosive and Besa into every crevice that attracted them, and the top of the ridge dissolved into a flying mass of flaking confetti as they did so.

D Company went in in two groups. Denis Hayward, Sergeant Morrisey and ten of our men as the forlorn hope, and Peter close supporting with the rest. Mike McDonald assaulted Butler's Hill at the same time, the first and last occasion when that nest of scorpions was ever subjected to such treatment.

Then the Inniskillings opened fire with their machine guns on the other side of Tangoucha, and sweeping the top of the col they followed up with smoke from their 2″ mortars over the whole of it.

The Germans on the hill fought it out like the rest of their comrades. They shot down half of A Company as Mike stormed over them ; the company carried the place within minutes though Mike himself was down with bullets through both legs.

On the ridge there was a longer but equally intense fire fight as our men of D Company crawled and clambered over the deadly rocks. Finally, coming to the glacis, Denis rushed it.

Peter Sillem, Corporal Willis and Rogan died in those moments. Fred Fincham and Heath were down mortally wounded, and others besides them. Then at the end, and all things ended, Corporal Swain and Fusilier Mallon were up – and on to the summit – in action with a solitary Bren.

These two, and five others of D Company, stood "Triumphant upon the fatal Hill" – but Napier was referring to the counter attack of our army at Albuera.

We were only a company. None the less our handful of Faughs carried the national honour with them, as well as that of our regiment.

The white flag went up.

Waved first over Point 622 ; the other defences followed. Then everywhere else in sight those listless emblems hung.

Here was the uttermost depth, the abject end of all things and the ultimate anticlimax.

As the tumult and the shouting died, the Captains, though hardly the Kings, took their leave.

Of the enemy thirty-six remained on their feet to surrender to Denis, and A Company added two dozen more. But we, their adversaries, had scarcely half that number left to receive them.

It was Easter Sunday.

15

Aftermath

No battle in the history of our regiment was attended by greater or more dramatic consequences than that of Kef el Tior, and none I fancy was ever fought out for a greater issue with such slender forces.

Dramatic then, it is historic now, and it fell to the Faughs to sever finally the defensive chain of those mountains – not by smiting the weakest link, but certainly the strongest. The result of it was immediate, and the German line whipped back in to fragments like a strand that had snapped under tension.

The enemy of course were approaching extremis anyway, with moral and spiritual factors creeping in to accelerate the collapse, but more important in those last days of April was the fact of their hill positions being tactically interdependent and impossible of defence in isolation. This accounted for the literal chain reaction that followed the battle. The most vital feature of all, Longstop Hill, that sinister custodian of the Medjez plain, owed its blood-stained tale just to this reason. But Longstop was now dominated and outflanked by the Irish Brigade, and Weber's last regiment threw in their hand twenty-four hours later after four days of murderous conflict with the rest of the 78th Division. That last barrier down, the entire Tunisian front caved in under the armoured onslaught that followed it.

Here, hidden in the story of these events, is the proof that the conduct of a few men at a point of supreme crisis can indeed affect the course of history and the fate of our country. Here was the reverse of Dunkirk, the worst defeat and greatest victory honoured impartially on our colours.

Our national history has of course been richly studded with like incidents, ever since Sir Richard Grenville set the pattern for conduct four centuries back. But never was this more true than during the long fight against Hitler's Germany. Our soldiers, like most of our countrymen, knew the stakes – and on 622 they knew too that those stakes were personal ones.

But what about our enemy. No one could doubt their resolution or valour. Unfortunately a mere examination of motives does not provide the whole reason for the performance of soldiers, though I think that evil causes fail in the end because in the last resort men will not sustain them.

However the professional spirit is a very strong one, and regular soldiers will fight to the end regardless of the cause they fight for. They have done so throughout all history. This underlay the performance of Koch's paratroopers as it always has done with German mercenaries, or ours for that matter, and no country is in less position to criticise than Ireland, who has given birth to so many of them. Our historic Irish Brigade, The Wild Geese, fought steadfastly in the worst of causes – not for freedom but to quell it and to extol aggression, for King Louis was not a shred different from Hitler save in refinement. Moreover at Malplaquet this self-same brigade was shot to bits and routed by the 18th Royal Irish, who were recruited from identical sources to themselves. These things merely prove that the professional spirit, mixed with veneration for the corps they belong to, counts for more with regular soldiers than all other factors put together, except for that Divine intangible, and patriotism which is sometimes part of it.

This brings us at last to Walter Koch's men, who were the best soldiers we encountered in Hitler's war and who were by no means destitute of religious faith. Heinz Preussner is adamant about his attitude. He did not like his country's conduct in Poland and Russia, but he was prepared to fight for his country and wanted, if not to win, at least to avoid losing, another war. A highly articulate and intelligent man, he said that he could not do less than join the most famous of the German regiments and, having done so, to put up the best performance that was in his power.

There is no doubt that he served under a great and inspiring leader in Walter Koch, and his motives should be respected.

In the last days the German army in Tunisia was desperate but it was not demoralised. As those grim days of April went by, neither food nor ammunition was coming into the country, and they knew that the game was up. Also, as usual in these circumstances, the jackals were out, and with no Germans safe in the part they occupied they needed half of their army to keep order behind the front. Their attenuated strength in their key mountain positions needs no further explanation.

Despite all, and with all lost, Koch's soldiers were committed to a last act of flamboyant defiance. They were called together by their C.O., Major Schirmer, and told that as they lacked the means to celebrate the Führer's birthday on 20 April they could get what they needed from the enemy. He thereupon loaded half a battalion of them on to the dozen or so surviving tanks of the 7th Panzers and set off up the glen until they encountered one of our artillery regiments. There they promptly surrounded the unfortunate gunners who, thinking the war already won, had omitted anything so tiresome as posting sentries. After a shortlived firework display the paratroopers withdrew, with a dozen or more of our vehicles and a large number of prisoners, mostly taken bloodlessly – in their pyjamas, as the final act of mortification, albeit salutary.

For his part in this raid by one unit of a beaten army which still retained its pride, Obergefreiter Heinz Preussner was awarded the Iron Cross, though Heinz remarked that the part he remembered best was ripping open an officer's tent and being told to "Go away, James, and stop making so much noise."

Most of our politicians and military commanders at the time seem to have regarded the result of the campaign in Tunisia as a foregone conclusion, though some of their writings make strange reading now. I think that one and all, save only our troops who were fighting them, consistently underestimated the enemy, and in the earliest phases this led to a reckless attitude which but for the intervention of the weather would have seen the ruin of our army.

There can be no doubt that the German strategic reasons for going in to Tunisia in November of 1942 were good ones, and in my opinion they could certainly have won – in the sense of securing their objectives for the duration and stale-mating the southern axis front. They could have turned the country in to an impregnable fortress and held it indefinitely.

Some of the reasons for their failure may appear here and there in this book, even if it is only the account of one infantry company that fought them.

One might ask how, and why, we won.

Most of us I believe felt that we had Divine power on our side, but I think also that our men fought harder than the Germans did – perhaps because of that power. I have often been asked how we would have fared defending those hills. Well, we had to twice, but I do not believe that if our soldiers had been defending the Tunisian mountains round Ang and Kef el Tior – those razor backs – that the enemy would ever have got us out of them. With the Germans the pitcher rarely returned twice to the same well ; when we hit them hard in our own defensive battles they usually went elsewhere. Our own army never did that. Stupid perhaps, but we persisted – and we persisted until our enemy could go on no longer. "Nous vaincerons parce que nous sommes le plus fort." The French used that expression in 1940, but then it was misapplied, and the Germans turned it to mockery against them. We could have said it though, for our mixture in the British Islands was more durable than either of those continental antagonists.

Our soldiers too were amply backed at home.

Fusilier Albert Heath, dying of his wounds, wrote back to his parents and said what we had tried to do for him. His mother, writing to me, said, ". . . but once again I thank you for all you done personaly and I am also glad that he played his part in that battle which you carried all before you. . . ."

And Mrs Hope, of her son who went down in that last rush for Point 622, ". . . we think perhaps the parting Words of his Dad had a lot to do with it. He just told him that now he was going out to fight for us – his home and be a soldier and be a man . . . it is such like lads that is going to take us right through. . . ."

Corporal James Given's father, carved from the same oak as his son, wrote similarly.

They all did.

Fusilier Spud Murphy, M.M., in hospital, wrote, "I consider it an honour to have served in the line with the regiment."

And Fanny Jefferies, mother of Nicolas, ". . . I am glad you were together . . . we were very proud of him. . . ."

But their letters were all like this, from all of our "Next of Kin". Their letters usually ended with their thoughts, and prayers – not for themselves but for us, and our regiment, and our safety. There were no atheists among our soldiers. Nor in their families either.

There was other correspondence of a different kind. Nelson said soothingly, "Your company is as well as can be expected without its oldest member . . . we are getting ready for the next item on the programme, for which we will always keep you a reserved (and front) seat."

And Denis Hayward wrote, "I am sending you the company roll herewith which will no doubt give you some shocks. . . . We late comers feel rather like new wine in old bottles – and definitely non-vintage."

My brother Michael from his nearby fighter bombers: "...owing to a slight miscalculation I flew into a trench...colossal black eye as I broke the reflector sight with my head; it's quite a stoutly built object. This was on the day after my birthday when I joined this circus... I should hate to be in Jerry's shoes... we are blowing him to pieces. I reckon Dunkirk must seem a plaything to Cape Bon just now . . . you realise what air superiority means when you see all our vehicles stooging forward unmolested pretty well head to tail . . . marvellous to be on the winning side this time . . . I suppose Dizzy [Desmond Gethin] was his usual splendid self. . . ."

My cousin James said sadly, "The worst thing that the 78th Division ever did was to get its reputation as hill fighters."

And writing home to my father, two weeks later, ". . . Journey down here was like a triumphal procession. Every station delightful. French folk produced coffee, chocolate cake, fruit, etc. Never known such a welcome and friendliness. There was a Guards lieutenant in with me who had lost a leg.

"The day before my misfortune I wrote to your Divisional

Petrol Officer and explained in the politest phrases I could think of what I thought of him and all his works. I hope his conscience may be pricked and that he will dish you out a few more coupons. I think sending you coupons to get to Leamington Station the height of impertinence." (Father was disabled at the time, J.H.C.H.)

"... It is rather a lovely place here. Beautiful flowers outside the window and birds shouting like hell all day. The only discordant note is during the night as there is a cat colony that conducts its love affairs about ten yards off in the garden.

"... It is a queer feeling being here while the grand climax of everything is taking place – like the left-behind feeling when one was a small child, or coming off at the last fence in a point to point. Am no lover of fighting but should have liked to have been in at the finish after all the sweat we have had. Still one can't grumble.

"It has been a peculiar country to fight in. . . . We have had to be mountaineers and we have even been fighting in the clouds. . . we understood none of the muleteers' lingo and they understood no English – wonderful confusion . . . they were good and went up the most incredible places.

"Those ridges were very difficult places to attack. Vertical faces along the sides, sometimes several hundred feet, and quite unclimbable with craggy spiky tops – with the top of the ridge itself only a few feet wide.

"Your regiment was always magnificent . . . we always found them most charming chaps to get on with. We usually had one of them living with us . . . and they have become close friends. I wonder if you would find things much different nowadays if you suddenly found yourself a battery commander again.

"It always seemed to me that the Germans were very different from those we met in France. They were all right until one got close to them and then very often they either ran for it or surrendered. Any fool can be brave behind a mortar, or a machine gun a thousand yards away.

"... I feel more charitably inclined to the ones who surrender without feeling the desire to further their country's cause first. The ones I like most are those charming individuals who walk blissfully in of an evening and announce their desertion, and how they hate the war and love the British.

"The Germans are queer folk. . . . We found them most entertaining – some were quite charming and great flatterers. They all said how fond they were of us . . . I never met one that wasn't delighted to be captured."

Returning two months later:

"It was like coming home again and have never known such a welcome. The Sergeants Mess held a terrific party and did their best to get me bottled. There were more of the old faces than I dared hope. My company got nine decorations . . . so we justified our existence. They tell me that the scenes in Tunis beggared description. No words on paper could have described it or what was entailed when an army a quarter million strong collapsed completely.

"The regiment is in marvellous form and of course morale is at a pinnacle. They are all looking immaculate – like peace-time soldiering to see their turn-out and bearing. Petty crime and the usual chaffs against discipline have disappeared because they have learned a new discipline and comradeship having all been through the mill together. I thought I should find the wreck of a regiment. . .

"Individuals I once thought worthless have something new in their characters they never had before too. Have had most wonderful letters from nexts of kin of my boys. They all reply when I write and without exception took it marvellously. They seem so delighted being written to . . . they have spirit.

"There are two very good chaps in D Company now. Bill Hanna and Denis Hayward – so they will be running the company from now on. I went to see Nicolas' grave which has been beautifully done and there is a chap that keeps fresh flowers on all of them."

Appendix A

STRICT COMPARISONS OF German and British military ranks are not possible due to the differing system of the two armies. In both world wars of this century the British army used the expedient of temporary rank, so that an officer normally carried the status of his appointment when he had been confirmed in it. For instance my substantive rank in Tunisia was lieutenant, although I held the title and pay of major.

The Germans did not follow this practice and they seem to have recognised substantive rank only. In consequence relatively junior officers were often found in important commands. Also the attached chart shows that the actual ranks of the two armies were not strictly comparable in respect of their functions.

It is important to note the structure of the German army so far as it concerns our history : a German division was more or less the same as our own. The Germans had the confusing habit in Africa of fighting in battle groups : Kampfgruppen, which took the name of the commander, like Oberstleutnant Koch's famous command, and which usually consisted of one or more infantry regiments with a variety of supporting arms.

The basic German infantry unit was the regiment, the equivalent of one of our brigades, and composed of three battalions, whereas in our own army individual battalions had regimental titles. German companies and sub units were bigger than ours.

In practice in this middle phase of the war, German regiments were usually commanded by oberstleutnants, and their battalions by majors or hauptmanns. Few infantry battalions in Tunisia had more than two or three senior officers and as often as not their companies were commanded by oberleutnants.

GERMAN MILITARY RANKS

Title	Usual Command	British equivalent
General Officers		
Generalfeldmarschall	Army Group	Field Marshal
Generaloberst	Army Group	No equivalent
General Der Infanterie, Panzertruppe, etc.	Army	General
Generalleutnant	Korps	Lieut. General
Generalmajor	Division	Major General
Officers		
Oberst	Regiment, often Division	Brigadier
Oberstleutnant	Regiment or Battalion	Lieut. Colonel
Major	Battalion or 2 i.c. Bn.	Major
Hauptmann	Kompanie or 2 i.c. Bn.	Captain
Oberleutnant	Kompanie	Captain or senior Lieut.
Leutnant	Zug Commander (platoon) or 2 i.c. Kompanie	Lieutenant or 2nd Lieut.
Unteroffiziers		
Hauptfeldwebel	Company Sergeant Major (Mother of the Company)	Warrant Offr. II
Feldwebel	Zug, 40 men, or 2 i.c. Zug	Warrant Offr. II
Unteroffizier	Gruppe or Section (dozen men) or 2 i.c. Zug (platoon)	Sergeant

Non Commissioned Officers		
Obergefreiter	Gruppe or 2 i.c. Gruppe. Usually assistant to Unteroffiziers	Corporal
Gefreiter	,, ,, ,,	Corporal. Two grades: over six years' service carrying extra stripe and much valued though not considered fit for further promotion
Oberschütze, Obergrenadier, etc.	Nil	Ranked as Fusilier but vested with authority

APPENDIX B

ORDER OF BATTLE 78th DIVISION
(major units only)

11 Infantry Brigade
- 2nd Bn. The Lancashire Fusiliers
- 1st Bn. The East Surrey Regiment
- 5th Bn. The Northamptonshire Regiment

36 Infantry Brigade
- 5th Bn. The Buffs (Royal East Kent Regiment)
- 6th Bn. The Queen's Own Royal West Kent Regiment
- 8th Bn. The Argyll and Sutherland Highlanders (Princess Louise's)

The Irish Brigade
- 6th Bn. The Royal Inniskilling Fusiliers
- 1st Bn. The Royal Irish Fusiliers (Princess Victoria's)
- 2nd Bn. The London Irish Rifles

56 Reconnaissance Regiment

1st Bn. Princess Louise's Kensington Regiment

Royal Artillery
- 17 Field Regiment
- 132 Field Regiment
- 138 Field Regiment
- 64 Anti Tank Regiment (Queen's Own Glasgow Yeomanry)
- 49 Light Anti Aircraft Regiment

Royal Engineers
- 214, 237 and 256 Field Companies
- 281 Field Park Company

Royal Army Medical Corps
- 11, 152 and 217 Field Ambulances

APPENDIX C

GLOSSARY

B.E.F.	British Expeditionary Force
Bn.	Battalion
Bofors	Light anti-aircraft gun. Equipment divisional L.A.A. regiment R.A.
Bren	Light machine gun. Magazine fed. Standard infantry weapon
Cdr.	Commander
Churchill	Heavy tank. Equipped with 6-pounder gun
C.O.	Commanding officer
Compo rations	Portable box of fourteen soldiers' rations for one day
C.Q.M.S.	Company Quartermaster Sergeant. The colour sergeant. The company's administrative N.C.O.
C.S.M.	Company sergeant major, who is a warrant officer
Djebel (Arabic)	Mountain
F.O.O.	Forward Observing Officer. Royal Artillery, usually with infantry forward troops
Faugh a Ballagh	Royal Irish Fusiliers regimental motto. Gaelic term. Actually Fág an Bealach, pronounced Fog a Bolla. Means "clear the way".
Faughs	Regimental nickname, Royal Irish Fusiliers
G.H.Q.	General Headquarters
Grant	Medium tank carrying 75 mm gun on starboard side. American built
Gruppe, (German)	Infantry section. Smallest sub unit. Usually a dozen men
H.Q.	Headquarters
I.O.	Intelligence Officer. Usually C.O.'s aide de camp in infantry battalions in action

I.C.	In command. 2 i.c. = second in command
Kompanie (German)	Infantry company. About 130 strong
K.S.L.I.	King's Shropshire Light Infantry
Medium (guns)	4.5 and 5.5 guns, or, German, 5.9s. Substantially heavier than the 25-pounder field artillery
Me.109 (German)	Messerschmitt fighter, or fighter bomber, aircraft
M.M.G.	Medium machine gun, e.g. German Spandau or British Vickers
M.O.	Regimental Medical Officer
M.T.	Motor transport
N.C.O.	Non-commissioned officer
O.P.	Observation post
Pl.	Platoon
Q.M.	Quarter Master, regimental supply officer, usually a captain
Q. Staff	Quartermaster staff, responsible for supply
R.A.	Royal Artillery
R.A.C.	Royal Armoured Corps
R.A.M.C.	Royal Army Medical Corps, to which the regimental doctor belonged
R.A.P.	Regimental Aid Post. The battalion medical centre operated by the regimental doctor and assisted by the medical sergeant
R.A.S.C.	Royal Army Service Corps. The divisional commissariat
R.Q.M.S.	Regimental quartermaster sergeant
Schmeisser (German)	Machine pistol. The equivalent of our tommy gun but superior in accuracy and reliability
Sherman	Medium tank carrying 75 mm gun in revolving turret. American built
Spandau (German)	Belt fed medium machine gun. Inferior to the Bren as an all purpose infantry weapon
S.P. Gun	Self propelled gun

Stick grenade (German)	Standard pattern grenade, German army
Stuka (German)	Dive bomber aircraft
Tommy gun	Sub machine gun, or machine carbine
Very light	White or coloured flare fired from pistol, for signalling or emergency illumination
Wadi (Arabic)	Water course. Usually refers to clefts in hillsides. Dry except in rainy season
Zug (German)	Infantry platoon of about forty men

Index

NOTE *Ranks mentioned are, generally, those applicable during the Tunisian campaign, or at the date of reference.*